ASSEMBLEDTOGETHER

the *POWER* of the local church

JOEL SIEGEL

Assembled Together – The Power of the Local Church
First Edition ©2014 Siegel Ministries, Inc.
Revised Edition ©2021 Siegel Ministries, Inc.

. . . . I am on fire with passion for your house.

John 2:17 (BBE)

Contents

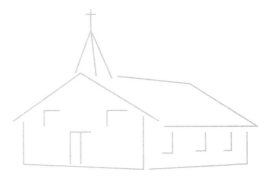

Chapter 1

Car Shopping

Many dread the day when they must shop for an automobile. Although I'm not a fan of the money games that some dealerships play, I mostly enjoy car shopping; I don't mind the process of dealing with salesmen or sitting at the negotiating table.

Manufacturers make several models of cars. Within each model, there are usually different sub-models or packages: collections of features that affect the functionality and price of the vehicle. Most cars are available in a base package: a budget-friendly, stripped-down model featuring only the most essential equipment. From there, one can select a variety of options designed to make the driving experience more convenient, safe, and pleasurable. Each of these options comes at a cost, but many are worth the cost. Shoppers must decide for themselves which options they need, and which might be more costly than they're worth.

Why all this talk about cars? The Body of Christ finds itself in a day when people treat Christianity like car shopping. You hear faith leaders talking about essentials and non-essentials: things that are necessary and things that are optional. Salvation, of course, would be considered essential, but many deem other parts of our faith non-essential. Personally, I can't bring myself to think this way. To me, everything God has provided for us is essential; nothing is non-essential or optional. I'm not interested in a stripped-down, no-frills kind of Christianity, yet it seems like many are.

When it comes to the subject of the local church, many treat it as non-essential: an available option that can be easily passed over. They consider their salvation experience to be Christianity's base package and think that if they have that they really don't need anything else. Nothing could be further from the truth. It's true that salvation (being born again) is most important and is the only thing that will get a person to Heaven. Christianity, however, includes so much more than our end-of-life trip to Heaven. God leaves us here on Earth after we're saved because He needs us here on Earth, involved with His plan. While the believer's salvation experience begins his or her Christian life, it's by no means all there is to the Christian life. There are a variety of aspects to our faith, none more central and essential than the local church.

When I bought my son his first vehicle, I could have saved thousands of dollars by purchasing the base model, but that model had no side airbags. A side-impact accident would have left my son exposed. Although the dealer offered these airbags as an option, I considered them to be a necessity. The protection of my family is worth the extra cost. Likewise, the benefits offered to the believer through the local church are priceless: worth any inconvenience or cost. The believer apart from the local church is like a passenger in an unsafe vehicle. They're exposed: an easy target for the enemy.

Why don't manufacturers make cars without brakes or headlights? Because those items are essential. One cannot safely operate an automobile and make progress without these vital components. In the same way, the local church is an essential part of Christianity. It's not safe to live as a Christian without the local church. Progress in one's life won't be realized without the local church. The church—*your* local church—is not just an available option, it's an absolute necessity.

If everyone had a healthy understanding of the place of the local church, there would be no need for books like this. Unfortunately, the Body of Christ finds itself lacking in understanding in this most important area.

Many of us have heard the phrase that says, "What you don't know can't hurt you." That's not true for the believer. When it comes to Bible subjects, including the subject of the local church, a lack of knowledge can cause a person to experience great difficulty. Don't settle for a life of ignorance and defeat. Don't be a minimalist Christian, driving the base model of your faith. Embrace every aspect of your life in Christ. Buy the good car!

God hasn't given you the spiritual equivalent of a rusted-out beater, He's given you a super-deluxe quality of life—loaded with all the bells and whistles. He's given you life. He's given you faith. He's given you the local church!

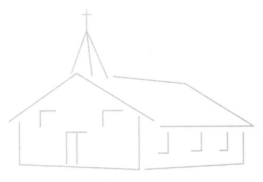

CHAPTER 2

Two Families

A day or two after completing this book, I received a phone call from a friend of mine who, more than anyone else, was used by God to lead me into a relationship with Christ. We had not spoken in several years, so I was glad to hear from him and was curious to know about the life he and his family were living. In his earlier years, he had been inconsistent in his walk with the Lord, so I wasn't sure what to expect when I asked him to fill me in on the details of his life.

I was blessed by what I heard. It seemed like every other sentence my friend spoke contained the phrase "my church."

This man and his family were thrilled to give large amounts of their time to serve in the ministries of their local church. He shared that his two eldest sons were avid soul-winners, both of whom were planning to train for ministry. I couldn't help but think about how different their story might have been had they not been so involved in their local church.

I then thought about a mutual friend of ours: the man who discipled me in the things of God when I was a new believer. This man and his family were the picture of stability as they gave themselves in service to God and remained active in their local church. Theirs was the first Christian marriage I had ever observed, and I paid close attention as I saw how they lovingly raised their young children.

I knew, however, that for the past twenty-five years or so, this man and his family had been out of church. He had become critical of his pastor's ministry and never seemed to be able to find another church for he and his family to attend. They eventually stopped looking.

Over the years, I watched as this man's children turned against him and his wife and turned against God. One child left the family and disappeared for a long season. The other found their place of acceptance in a homosexual relationship. This man and his wife have endured great hardship, living year after year with intense physical and financial challenges. They rarely see their children and hardly know their grandchildren.

Both families are dear to me. I could never repay them for their godly influence in my life at a time when I was vulnerable and impressionable. Did God just see fit to bless the one family and curse the other? Not at all. The outcome of their lives is nothing more than a reflection of their connection with the local church. God loves both families equally, but simply cannot help the one who refuses their place of help.

These two families represent many thousands of families within the Body of Christ today. Some avail themselves of the power of the local church, while others think it unnecessary to assemble together. Which kind of person are you? The outcome of your life depends on what you do with the local church.

CHAPTER 3

God's Plan for Today

When sports teams prepare for the next game on their schedule, they don't just go through basic drills and workouts. They game-plan for the specific team they're going to meet. While maintaining their skills in a general sense, they also make preparation specific to their opponent. Any good coach begins with a game plan: the team's blueprint for victory.

God's a master planner. There's nothing random about the way He works; He works according to His own plan. His plan, however, cannot be fulfilled without the cooperation and participation of those in His Body. The Body of Christ must discover and follow God's plan as revealed in the pages of Scripture. Details of His plan—things He desires to emphasize at certain strategic times—must also be discerned and cooperated with. God often reveals these details to those who have prominent places of leadership within the Body.

I was privileged to travel for several years with one such leader: Rev. Kenneth E. Hagin. Brother Hagin's ministry had a massive reach, influencing leaders and believers throughout the world. One benefit I enjoyed as part of his ministry team was sitting in all of his services. Being with him on a regular basis gave me an advantage, in that I was able to hear not just the variety of truths that he preached, but also the repetition of those truths. The things that he spoke over and over were the things he was trying to most emphasize. The casual or infrequent listener might have heard what was being said but would not be able to recognize the level of emphasis that came through repetition.

In almost every series of meetings, Brother Hagin would share one particular thought. As people would ask him, "What's God doing today?" he would always respond with this answer: "In our day, God's endeavoring to establish strong local churches that know how to flow with the Holy Spirit." Brother Hagin emphasized the place of the local church because he had discovered the truth that God's plan is the local church.

His was not the kind of flashy answer that most people

wanted. People are always more excited about topics such as demonic deliverance, visions and revelations, and healing and miracles than they are about something as seemingly mundane as the local church. It must be understood, however, that without the local church, none of the so-called "exciting things" I just mentioned would happen with much effectiveness.

Does Scripture support this emphasis on the local church? Decidedly, yes. When Paul embarked on his missionary journeys, his focus was on planting and developing local churches. God's plan has always been the local church.

> And when they had appointed elders for them in every church, with prayer and fasting they committed them to the Lord in whom they had believed.
>
> Acts 14:23

A MEETING I'LL ALWAYS REMEMBER

When the time came for myself and my family to leave Brother Hagin's ministry to plant our first church, I requested a few minutes of his time in order to submit my ministry plans to him. I had worked as part of his crusade team for several years and, as a matter of honor and respect, was interested in making sure he was in agreement with my plans to leave (it's always right to seek the counsel of our elders, especially our pastor, when making major decisions. Brother Hagin had about a half-century more experience than I did in ministry. Although I felt I had heard from God, I valued any confirmation or instruction I might receive from him).

After hearing my plans, Brother Hagin began to speak to me about some things that would have to happen in order for God's end-time plan to come to pass. In particular, he talked about the many churches that would have to be raised up: storehouses where God could safely put His harvest. He went on to say, "That's why God led us to start Rhema" (Rhema Bible Training College, the school he founded in the 1970s). Our meeting lasted about 45 minutes (he did almost all the talking), and once again I could see just how much emphasis he placed upon the local church.

Brother Hagin's statement describing God's activity in our day agrees with the Word of God. The prophet Isaiah foretold the importance of the local church in the last days. Although the term *church* wasn't used then, he spoke of the prominence of God's *house*. Old Testament references to God's house, temple, or Mount Zion can be symbolic of the New Testament church (see 1 Timothy 3:15 and Hebrews 12). Here's that passage in Isaiah:

> In the last days, the mountain of the Lord's house
> will be the highest of all—**the most important place**

on earth. It will be raised above the other hills, and people from all over the world will stream there to worship. People from many nations will come and say, "Come, let us go up to the mountain of the Lord, to the house of Jacob's God. There he will teach us his ways, and we will walk in his paths." For **the Lord's teaching will go out from Zion**; his word will go out from Jerusalem.

Isaiah 2:2-3 (NLT)

What a tremendous passage! The local church in the last days is the most important place on Earth. Churches today often live stream their services, but notice the emphasis of this passage. People aren't to just sit at home watching the church's video stream. *They*—people from every nation—are to stream to their local churches to worship and receive teaching from the Lord. Notice also that people in the last days are to enthusiastically invite others, saying, "Come on, let's go to church!" There's nothing more exciting than the activity of the local church, and there's nothing that God is emphasizing today more than the local church.

Brother Hagin's answer to the question of what God is doing in our day was not something he thought of off the top of his head. He sought the Lord (and His Word) and waited upon Him for His answer. It's interesting that the Lord didn't just speak of establishing churches, He specified *strong* local churches.

STRONG LOCAL CHURCHES

> And he passed through Syria and Cilicia, establishing and **strengthening the churches.**
>
> Acts 15:41 (AMP)

Not every church is a strong church. Some churches grow in strength initially, but later weaken by conforming to the world instead of following the plan of God. God's not interested in a network of weak churches, yet the majority of churches in our cities and towns are weak, and some, sadly, are dead.

Who decides whether a church is weak or strong? God, of course, sees these things most clearly, but He also gives us insight from His Word, enabling us to make sound judgements for ourselves. The terms *weak* and *strong*, as used in the New Testament, refer to spiritual strength and effectiveness. We don't just look at natural indicators to assess spiritual strength. Numbers don't always equal strength, nor do buildings, ministry outreaches, staff members, or television programs. When God speaks of strong and weak, He's speaking in spiritual terms. It takes spiritual strength to make spiritual progress.

Jesus once told his disciples that He had things to say to them that they could not yet bear (John 16:12). They couldn't bear (or receive) them because they weren't yet strong enough to receive them. They wouldn't be able to receive these deeper truths until they were born again and could grow spiritually. In a similar example, the writer of Hebrews chastised his readers for being dull of hearing (Hebrews 5:11). Theirs wasn't an issue of physical hearing loss, rather they were too spiritually weak to grasp the truth. It's possible for people to be spiritually weak when they ought to be strong.

> For even though by this time you ought to be teaching others, you actually need someone to teach you over again the very first principles of God's Word. You have come to need milk, not solid food.
>
> Hebrews 5:12 (AMP)

All these Christians could handle was an eye-dropper full of milk. No one can grow strong on just a little milk, nor can a church be considered strong if its attendees never grow past spiritual infancy. God's emphasis in our day is the establishment of strong local churches. Regardless of age or size, a church must develop spiritually in order to be strong. Yes, we want to reach people and win the lost, but that alone won't result in a spiritually robust church. Believers of all ages must be nurtured and discipled so that they may grow.

Let's make spiritual strength our focus. Let's have the growth and increase that comes from God and we'll enjoy the greatness of His blessing.

MAKING MOVEMENT WITH GOD

When the Lord shared with Brother Hagin His plan for strong local churches, He identified one particular characteristic that would qualify a church as being strong. The strong church is one that knows how to flow with the Spirit of God. It's a church where the entire congregation (not just the minister) has learned to make spiritual movement together. If churches are to follow God's plan, people must be taught to move and flow with God. It's regrettable that not every pastor trains their congregations in these things. Perhaps the pastors themselves don't yet know how to flow with the Holy Spirit, but all can learn. This knowledge is not some sovereign gift bestowed only upon a select few, but is a learned skill that anyone can acquire.

The thought of a worldwide network of churches flowing with the Spirit causes our enemy to exert full effort to diminish the Church's place. The enemy greatly fears the church that understands the flow of God, for when a congregation moves with God as one, God's purposes are unhindered and His will accomplished. How tragic that many churches remain ignorant of God's flow, and some even oppose the moving of His Spirit. In my ministry travels, I've found very few churches where the people know how to flow with the Spirit of God.

Let's commit to following God's plan for our day, and let's hunger for the flow of God in our midst, following those in leadership as they direct us in skillful movement. Individually and collectively, we must strive for proficiency in the things of God. As we do, our churches will become the kind that God regularly visits with manifestations of His presence and power. Like God, we must be committed to establishing strong local churches that know how to flow with the Spirit.

CHAPTER 4

The Local Church in Scripture

Not neglecting to meet together, as is the habit of some, but encouraging one another, and all the more as you see the Day drawing near.

Hebrews 10:25

There are some verses in the Bible that require plenty of explanation if the meaning is to be understood, but that's not the case here. This verse stands alone with a message that's clear and bold: *get to church and stay in church!* Many believers are familiar with this great verse, but I believe its scriptural significance is overlooked.

THE GREATEST BOOK OF THE BIBLE?

Perhaps you've heard stories from foreign lands where Bibles were scarce and people had been waiting for years to read God's Word. When a copy finally arrived, it would be torn apart, book by book, so it could be distributed throughout the community. I know, it's not fair for one person to get the Gospel of John and another person to go home with nothing but Ecclesiastes, but presumably everyone would have the chance to read all sixty-six books. What a precious sight it must be to God for there to be such hunger for His Word.

If you could only have one of the sixty-six books of the Bible, which would you choose? Perhaps you've never pondered that question, but I have. I would select the book of Hebrews. I know that's an interesting choice, given the mystery that surrounds the book's authorship, but there's an important reason why I would pick Hebrews.

The book of Hebrews is sort of like the whole Bible in one book. It teaches many major doctrines, gives plenty of Old Testament background, lifts the veil of the spirit realm, and shows the transition from Old to New Covenant. It reveals both the earthly and heavenly ministry of Jesus, explains the many benefits of our inheritance in Christ, and contains truth found nowhere else. All that, and there's also plenty of practical instruction, as well as the most famous chapter in the Bible on faith. That Hebrews was chosen to be included in the New Testament Canon without the required provenance is a testimony to the richness of its content. It's a very significant book in the Bible.

I mentioned that our text, Hebrews 10:25, stands alone. While it's true that this verse is easily understood by itself, there's really no such thing in the Bible as a verse that stands alone. Every verse in the Bible is subject to its surrounding context. (This is a widely accepted rule of Bible interpretation.) The rest of the passage, the rest of the chapter, and even the rest of the book must be considered when defining the full meaning and importance of a verse. As we consider the surrounding verses, we see that Hebrews 10:25 doesn't just derive its importance from what it says, it's also important because of where it is.

A LESSON IN LITERATURE AND MUSIC

As you read through the book of Hebrews, you find layer upon layer of truth set in place to form the framework of the book. Works of literature (like the Bible) are similar to works of music in that they build and take shape as they progress.

When listening to a symphony, one could draw along on a sheet of paper, creating a timeline that looks similar to a mountainous landscape. On that timeline, one would see the ebb and flow of the composition: tension and release, loud versus soft, the expected and the unexpected, themes and variations, and so on. These elements lead to what's called the climax: the part where the music comes together (the peak of the mountain). There are often several climactic moments in a musical composition, but just one that would be considered the main climax, usually about three quarters of the way through the piece.

In a literary composition, the climax would be the part of the writing that takes all the previous thoughts and puts them together to make the one main point. This is best seen in the book of Hebrews by reading the entire book through in one sitting. In my opinion, the climax of the book of Hebrews is a passage found in the tenth chapter. Since the book of Hebrews is a condensed version of the entire Bible, we could expect the climax to be a summary of the Bible's main themes (redemption and its benefits are the main themes of the Bible). That's exactly the case with Hebrews. Here's that climactic passage—a single paragraph:

> Therefore, brothers, since we have confidence to enter the holy places by the blood of Jesus, by the new and living way that he opened for us through the curtain, that is, through his flesh, and since we have a great priest over the house of God, let us draw near with a true heart in full assurance of faith, with our hearts sprinkled clean from an evil conscience and our bodies washed with pure water. Let us hold fast

the confession of our hope without wavering, for he who promised is faithful. And let us consider how to stir up one another to love and good works, not neglecting to meet together, as is the habit of some, but encouraging one another, and all the more as you see the Day drawing near.

Hebrews 10:19-25

In this passage we see it all: God's faithfulness, what Jesus has done (and is now doing) for us, who we have become, what we can do, our responsibilities toward God, others, etc. The first several verses describe the unrestricted access to God that's been made available to us. The last verse, however, gives us the key to successfully enjoying that access. We must *not neglect to meet together* if we are to draw near, operate in faith, speak the right things, properly relate to others, etc. In this premier scripture passage, verses 19-24 tell us the *what*, but verse 25 tells us the *how*. The local church is the *how*; the local church is the key.

What's more important, the car or the keys? Neither one by itself can accomplish anything, but it's the keys that unlock the potential of the car, allowing progress to be made. No keys, no movement. Nothing is more holy and precious than the blood that secured our redemption, but the local church provides the key to understanding that redemption, as people are taught and enlightened. Could we not say that the most important verse in this passage is the verse that gives us the key that mobilizes all the rest? Everything that Jesus has done for us comes together in the local church.

Think about how significant this is. The most important verse in the most important passage in one of the most important books of the Bible speaks of the local church.

Many have overlooked the level of emphasis that the Bible places on the local church. The Holy Spirit is the One who connected the local church with some of the most fundamental parts of our faith. Were the local church any less important, its mention would be out of place in this pivotal New Testament passage. God has given the local church a place of supreme emphasis in His Word; we must adopt thinking in line with that emphasis.

THE CLIMAX AFTER THE CLIMAX

Prior to the ending of a musical composition, there's often a section that revisits the climax and restates the theme. This section is called the *recapitulation*. It's sort of like what I sometimes do at dinner. I act as though I'm done for a while, but then I scoop out just enough food for a few more bites. I *recap* my dinner. Chapter ten of Hebrews brings the themes of the book together for a triumphant climax, but in chapter twelve there is another climax—a few more bites—summarizing all that's been discussed.

But you have come to Mount Zion and to the city of
the living God, the heavenly Jerusalem, and to myr-
iads of angels, to **the general assembly and church
of the firstborn** who are enrolled in heaven, and to
God, the Judge of all, and to the spirits of the righteous made perfect, and to Jesus, the mediator of a
new covenant, and to the sprinkled blood, which
speaks better than the blood of Abel.

Hebrews 12:22-24 (NASB)

There's an obvious similarity between this passage and the
one we studied in Hebrews chapter ten. Both mention the
church while speaking of some of the other most sacred aspects of our faith. The church is listed here in the same company as the Blood of Christ, the Judgement Seat of Christ,
and the entire angelic host. It sounds important to me.

What's interesting about this passage in Hebrews chapter
twelve is how the reference to the whole church reads in the
original language. It literally reads this way: *all the called-out
ones assembled together.* Wow! That gives us an even more
clear picture of the Church. The local church would be all
the called-out ones in a particular community assembled
together. Notice it doesn't say *a tenth of the called-out ones
assembled together.* Nor does it say *all the called-out ones
watching online.* We must all physically assemble in our local
church on a regular basis.

Each of these two climactic passages in Hebrews mentions the Church's gathering together. Those who refuse to gather together in their local church will be in for a shock on the day when we're all gathered together to meet the Lord in the air (2 Thessalonians 2:1). In one sense, our times of gathering here on Earth are rehearsals for the day when we're gathered together to meet Him in Heaven.

The place of the local church in the believer's life simply cannot be overstated. The prominence it's given in God's Word shows that, without the local church, the believer has little chance of enjoying the full benefits of his or her redemption. Today's take-it-or-leave-it attitude toward the local church is in sharp contrast to the passages we've seen in Hebrews. The view of the local church in our day must change to match the emphasis seen in God's Word.

CHAPTER 5

Neglect

Not neglecting to meet together, as is the habit
of some, but encouraging one another, and all the
more as you see the Day drawing near.

Hebrews 10:25

Do we really believe the Bible? Are we truly committed
to obedience? If we answered that question by observing the church attendance of the Body of Christ, we would
conclude that most Christians neither believe nor obey the
Word. Scripture is clear as to the level of involvement each
believer is to have with his or her local church: all the way

in. Many people neglect their local church. They have a variety of ways by which they justify their disobedience of God's command to meet together.

When this verse speaks of meeting together, it's not talking about meeting for coffee, or to play volleyball. Our spiritual success hinges on our meeting together for worship. Although personal interaction and fellowship activities are valuable, this verse is speaking primarily of public worship in the local church. Other translations help clarify this:

> Not forsaking or neglecting **to assemble together** [as believers], as is the habit of some people, but admonishing (warning, urging, and encouraging) one another, and all the more faithfully as you see the day approaching. (AMP)

> Let us not neglect **our church meetings**, as some people do, but encourage and warn each other, especially now that the day of his coming back again is drawing near. (TLB)

The primary way people neglect their church is by failing to attend church. When new believers see other church members attending sporadically, they take their cue and do the same. When leadership fails to emphasize the necessity of frequent and regular attendance, people assume that everyone (including God) is okay with an anything-goes attitude. Although the world may live by the phrase *whatever works for you*, the Church is to live by *every word that proceeds from the mouth of God* (Matthew 4:4). God's Word tells us to assemble together. That's the word we'll live by. We gather because we're commanded to.

God is grieved and His will and plan hindered when people neglect His church. Let's obey the Bible and make the local church our priority. Not seeing the local church as God sees it—as an important and weighty thing—is a main reason people don't give the church its due respect. A lack of respect is the root of neglect. If you respect the church, you won't neglect the church.

EXCUSES, EXCUSES

The reasons why Christians miss church are numerous. As a pastor for many years, I heard most (if not all) the excuses out there. Of course, there are some valid reasons why a believer might occasionally miss a service, but many are habitually absent, neglectful of the place of the local church in their lives.

In some cases, I can understand the Christian who desires to skip church. I've been to a lot of churches, and would have difficulty regularly attending some of them. If I went to a restaurant and the food and service were lousy, I wouldn't become a regular customer. Likewise, if I attend a service where I'm not spiritually fed, or everything is disorganized and haphazard, I'll be in a hurry to leave and won't want to return. Sadly, some churches aren't worth attending.

There's a type of church in our day that's popular, new, and exciting, but from a spiritual standpoint, lacking. I call these churches "false churches."

The false church is one where the things of God are imitated in the flesh rather than presented genuinely in the spirit. I don't mean that the members are unsaved, or that the leaders are insincere. They may be decent, God-loving people but are missing certain key elements as they worship. Although the false church may have an appearance of godliness, their services lack power (see 2 Timothy 3:5). Entertainment and convenience have replaced anointing and substance. Rather than catering to the desires of the Spirit, they cater to the comfort of people's flesh. The intention of these churches may be good, but they have very little fruit to show for their efforts.

These false churches (or "flesh" churches) have sprung up around the world in large number. The false church doesn't deliver enough spiritual substance to people to help them develop the habit of coming hungry and often. Attending there is like going out for dinner but only being served candy. Because the false church is now the mainstream church, the poor attendance habits of their members are setting the trends.

The church I attended as a young believer had three services per week. I attended them all (as did the majority of our congregation). Today, instead of attending three times a week, the trend is for people to attend only once or twice a month. People think that by showing up every third or fourth Sunday they're acceptably serving God, but that's not so. They may feel as though God's in agreement with their sporadic attendance, and that He understands and condones the fact that they so often miss worship. They're mistaken. God is grieved by this kind of neglect. Many of these believers simply don't know any better and must be taught.

I DIDN'T MAKE IT

Leaders in churches often hear their people say, "Sorry, I didn't make it to the service" or "I'm not sure if I can make it or not." What's that supposed to mean? You didn't make it because you didn't plan to. You never started out. Never got out of bed, never got dressed, never got in the car, never headed down the road. Of course you didn't make it. We've never "not made it" when we headed toward our church. We've been hindered or delayed a few times by snow. Perhaps once or twice a car wouldn't start because of a dead battery, but we still eventually made it. If someone calls their employer and says, "I don't think I'll make it today," it had better mean there's a big issue, like a severe sickness. Most people would never bring the same excuses to their job that they bring to their local church. Is work more important than church? It shouldn't be.

"Well, I get compensated for being at work. I don't at church." That's where you're wrong. You may not draw a paycheck from your church, but make no mistake: many of God's rewards for your life are contingent upon your involvement in your local church. There's indeed rich compensation for your attendance and involvement.

What's the best excuse you've heard for disobeying Hebrews 10:25? Car trouble? Helping a friend move? Sporting event? Work schedule? Demonic oppression and warfare? I've heard all of these, but the excuse I heard most often had to do with family obligations. People seem to believe that family trumps church every time. "My nephew had a ball game I had to attend." You had a meeting with God you were supposed to attend. "We had a family gathering." You missed your worship gathering. Are these excuses valid? It depends on how much value one places on the local church. I've chosen to agree with God's Word instead of conforming to the thinking of today's Christians.

I won't help you move on Sunday morning. If my car won't start, I'll call someone to come get me. I'm not regularly coming into work on Sunday morning. If the devil is pestering me at home, let's all go to church and see how he likes it there. I'm not missing church for anyone or anything (except a genuine emergency), because I understand the importance and place of the local church.

GOD AND FAMILY

Let's talk more about family obligations. One of the biggest lies that modern believers have accepted is that family is the most important thing there is. That's a dangerous falsehood because it involves a truth that's being stretched too far. Family *is* important, but putting family before God pushes the importance of family beyond its rightful place. It's important for parents to spend time with their kids, but never are children or one's spouse more important than serving God. The local church is the main avenue through which the entire family serves the Lord.

"Nothing's more important than family" is a favorite saying in our day. Says who? God's more important than your family. You wouldn't have a family without Him, and you sure couldn't keep one together without Him. Family activities do not justify neglect of the local church. People fabricate excuses to remove themselves from the anointing that brings correction and help to their lives. The devil loves these kinds of people because they make his job so easy. He doesn't want anyone present where God is moving.

Don't allow family functions to keep you away from the

things of God. It's unnecessary for your children to participate in every activity that exists. It *is* necessary that they're
taught not to participate in things that conflict with church.
Signing up children for a softball league (or football, soccer,
ballet, etc.) on Sunday mornings is one of the biggest mistakes a parent can make. These games can be played at other
times, not during church.

The dad who frequently misses church to go hunting or
fishing is setting the wrong example for his children. Recreational activities are okay at the right time, but not when
it's church time. Dad, you'll regret those hunting and fishing
trips later on when you're watching your children struggle to
keep their families together. Your children will follow your
example.

Most of us have heard the saying, "Children won't do as
you say, they'll do as you do." There's truth to that. A friend
of mine recently heard a parent scolding their teenage child
for smoking. That parent had a lit cigarette in her hand the
whole time. One has to be blind not to see that words mean
nothing in those situations.

I remember a lady in our church who would attend on
Sundays, but would come to us whenever we had a special
event to say that she wouldn't be there because of a family
obligation. (People think that if they inform their pastor of
their absence it's excused, but that doesn't mean God excuses
it.) I never spoke to her about this issue, but I watched as this

lady—who had been saved and Spirit-filled in our church—eventually removed herself altogether from our ministry. She moved on to a church where nothing much was expected of the attendees and where there was no manifestation of the things of God. On her way out, she influenced a few others to follow her. Those kinds of decisions will bring regret.

I realize that some churches schedule activities every night of the week in order to accommodate different interest groups and meet different needs. I'm not suggesting that a person is to neglect their family in order to attend every function of a large, busy church. My point is, when the pastor has been led to schedule services, including the regular weekly meetings, God expects you to be there to the degree possible. It's so important that we regularly meet together.

TAKING A BREAK FROM CHURCH

The excuses that some people fabricate to stay out of church are beyond belief. One of the craziest is when people say they need to "back off for a while," "take a break," or "take a vacation from church." They fail to understand that to back off from the church in which God placed them is to back off from Him. We're never to take a break from God. While it's true that some people sign up for too many jobs at church, it's never right to "take a vacation from church." (I'm talking about people who stay at home one Sunday each month for a vacation from church, not those who are actually away on vacation.) Staying at home is not vacation, it's rebellion (old-time believers called it *backsliding*). People use these excuses to pull away from church and then, when their family falls apart, they blame it on the church. I resent that. Serving in the local church has never yet split a family apart.

I once had a church member tell me that God was instructing them to stay away from church in order to protect their family. They were listening to the wrong god! The god of this world (Satan) will tell you to leave church in order to protect your family. The God of the Bible will tell you to get *in* church in order to protect your family. If something's really going on at a church that's harmful to families, please inform the pastor. If he or she won't listen, inform those to whom the pastor is accountable. That way the problem can be stopped before the local church ends up on the local news.

MEDIUM GRAY DAYS

One of the great things about Heaven is the perpetually temperate climate (at least I hope that's the case). It will need to be nice because, if the weather is bad and people in Heaven act like they do on Earth, Jesus won't have much of a crowd for worship. I have a name for believers who are picky about things like the weather. I call them *Goldilocks*

Christians. In the tale of *Goldilocks and the Three Bears,* everything had to be just right or she wouldn't accept it. Never mind that she wasn't paying for anything—she was actually breaking and entering—the soup, mattress, chair etc. had to be perfect.

Goldilocks Christians demand that the sound system be the perfect volume, the children's workers be able to always keep their child calm, the pastor preach a message that's just right in length, and the weather always be favorable. As a minister who has pioneered more than one church, I've learned to use my faith to keep the Goldilocks Christians away, and to bring those who have a pioneering spirit alongside to help us.

You can accommodate Goldilocks Christians in some areas, but it's hard to control the weather. I pastored for many years in a part of the country that had a lot of snow, and only about sixty days of sunshine per year. I found that there were two main times when people wouldn't come to church: when the weather was bad and when the weather was nice. If snow was coming down on a Sunday morning (or any time during the previous 24 hours), a pastor would be in trouble, because the idea of church is not exciting enough for some people to go out and clear the snow.

The other kind of weather we didn't want on a Sunday morning was a nice day with sunshine. Because sunny days were rare, church-goers had difficulty not being lured away by the sun. My wife and I figured out how to apply our faith to this dilemma. We began to thank God for something we called "medium gray days." Not too snowy, not too sunny. Just overcast enough to get the people to church.

We can all see how silly this is. Pastors shouldn't have to use their faith to keep the weather from being nice. Believers must understand the importance of the local church, being so committed to their place, that it would take a major event to keep them away. May we all be people who share God's love for the local church.

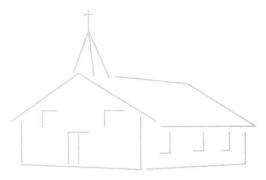

CHAPTER 6

Habits

Not neglecting to meet together, **as is the habit of some**, but encouraging one another, and all the more as you see the Day drawing near.

Hebrews 10:25

People are creatures of habit. Whether good or bad, habits can be formed in different areas of one's life. The best and most important habit anyone can develop is the church habit. The habit of being at church is more important than the habit of brushing your teeth (although everyone at church will appreciate that you brush your teeth). Toothpaste protects your teeth but church protects your life. The most important habit any parent can teach their children is the habit of serving in the local church. Instilling this habit in a child is the parent's responsibility. It's not the job of the grandparents to pick up their grandkids and take them to church while the parents sleep in.

People don't just need church habits, they need good church habits. It doesn't just matter *that* you come; it matters *how* you come. It matters what you do when you arrive. When we're driving to church, whether as ministers or attendees, we direct our hearts toward the Lord. Our kids know that the drive to church, pleasant though it may be, won't be filled with a lot of small talk and goofing around. That can happen later. We have important business to prepare for on the way to church.

Develop the habit of arriving early rather than late. Regularly arriving late to church shows that a person doesn't properly value the church. It's ironic that people are okay with showing up late for a worship service, but they get agitated if they miss even one preview at the movie theater. People routinely waltz in twenty minutes late to church and think nothing of it. Some of them, I'm certain, do it for attention, hoping that others will turn around to look at them. If they pulled that kind of stunt at their job, there would be severe consequences.

I used to teach our people about the "first-song blessing."

I told them that God moved in a special way for those that were there for the first song (the beginning of the service). Yes, I made up that doctrine, but it got my point across. And besides, it's true that those who are diligent to be where God wants them will be blessed in greater ways than those who are loose with their attendance.

JESUS' CUSTOM

> And he came to Nazareth, where he had been brought up. And **as was his custom**, he went to the synagogue on the Sabbath day, and he stood up to read.
>
> Luke 4:16

One reason Jesus could be so mightily used of God was that He had been well prepared for ministry throughout the course of His life. Part of that preparation included the worship habits that His earthly parents had given Him. He was so in the habit of being at church that when He became separated from His parents on a trip, they were able to find Him by going to the house of God.

> And when he was twelve years old, they went up **according to custom**. And when the feast was end-

ed, as they were returning, the boy Jesus stayed behind in Jerusalem. His parents did not know it, but supposing him to be in the group they went a day's journey, but then they began to search for him among their relatives and acquaintances, and when they did not find him, they returned to Jerusalem, searching for him. After three days **they found him in the temple**, sitting among the teachers, listening to them and asking them questions.

Luke 2:42-46

If someone didn't know where to find you, where would they think to look? Many people have a regular seat at the local bar, or a place on the golf course or basketball court. I enjoy some recreational activities, but those places aren't where you should look for me. If I'm not home and the church is meeting, that's where you'll find me.

He said, "Why were you looking for me? Didn't you know that **I had to be here**, dealing with the things of my Father?" But they had no idea what he was talking about.

Luke 2:49-50 (MSG)

Notice in this passage that Jesus said, "I had to be there." We've developed good church habits when we, like Jesus, feel as though we have to be there every time the doors are open—not because it's an obligation, but because it's an opportunity! Jesus and His family had the custom of going to the place of worship, even when it was a days-long journey. A custom is something that's become a habit in one's life. Many have developed the habit of neglecting the local church, but that habit can be changed into the habit of regular care for the local church. We'd all like to experience results in life like Jesus experienced, but to duplicate His results, we must duplicate His habits.

CHANGING MY BAD HABITS

The way to develop a good habit is to make a commitment (a quality decision) to the behavior you want to develop. Write it down, declare it, and allow no exceptions while the habit is being formed. There have been times in my life when I've had to replace bad habits with good ones, and this is how I did it. For years, I had ignored my dentist's recommendation to floss. I didn't think my lack of flossing would affect my oral health (as the dentist had warned), but when I returned every six months for a visit, my mouth would be a mess; blood from my gums would be everywhere.

I realized that this scene wasn't the dentist's fault; it was my fault for ignoring his counsel. After one particularly rough visit, I decided that things were going to change—I was going to become a daily flosser. I don't remember how long ago that was, but I've flossed for so long now that a visit to the dentist hardly bothers me. My good habits have yielded good results. The habit that has produced the greatest results, however, is my church habit. I wouldn't know what to do with myself on a Sunday morning other than go to church.

MISSING GOD FOR A DOG

My family and I live in an area where outdoor activities abound, and people are committed to every kind of hobby and pastime you could imagine. As an example, people in my town just adore their dogs. I don't mean they adore them the way normal people enjoy pets; they love their dogs the way Hindus worship cows. Every town in my area has at least one full-service pet spa, complete with bakery (because no dog should have to eat treats out of a box).

On my way to church on Sunday mornings I pass dog parks: the busiest places in town. People there think they're training their dogs, but they don't realize that their dogs are training them: giving them the habit of missing worship. I have nothing against dogs. We have one that we enjoy, but my dog will not keep me from serving God. He can sit at home by himself for hours while we're at church. People all over the world are missing out on G-o-d because of a d-o-g.

That's backward. I refuse to go to hell for a dog!

Develop the habit of consistent church attendance. Get used to arriving early, not rolling in late. Find areas in which to serve and make serving your priority.

Many couples have this conversation on Saturday evenings: "What do you think about church tomorrow? Do you want to go, or do we have other things to do?" That's a conversation you'll never hear at my house and it's a conversation no believer should have. Are they having church? Then I'll be there. It's my custom. It's automatic. It's priority. It's my habit.

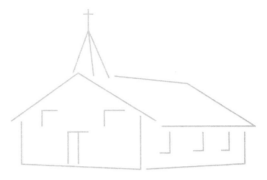

CHAPTER 7

One Another

Not neglecting to meet together, as is the habit of
some, but encouraging one another, and all the
more as you see the Day drawing near.

Hebrews 10:25

The believer's involvement in his or her local church is
not just for their own benefit. We're all members of the
Body of Christ, each member having responsibilities toward
the others. No part of my physical body functions independently of the other parts, nor do I function in the Body
of Christ independently of the other members. For the plan

of God to come to pass on the Earth, there must be real-time interaction between the members of Christ's Body.

God takes the members of His Body and places them in a local body: the local church. Each church functions as a family, with individual members sharing in the responsibilities and enjoying the benefits. While we recognize that the local church should reach out beyond its four walls, we must not diminish the value of the church's ministry to its own members. How is that ministry accomplished? By the activities of both the pastor and the members. The pastor takes the lead in ministry, but all are to share the responsibility of ministering to one other.

The New Testament teaches this responsibility of each member toward the others. Below are quotations from the letters of Paul, Peter, James, and John. Notice how many times the phrase *one another* is used, and what our ministry to those among us is to look like.

We are to:

- serve one another
- greet one another
- comfort one another
- care for one another
- instruct one another
- welcome one another
- love one another (mentioned over a dozen times)

- show kindness to one another
- live in harmony with one another
- submit to one another
- teach and admonish one another
- encourage one another
- do good to one another
- exhort one another
- stir up one another
- confess our sins to one another
- show hospitality to one another
- clothe ourselves with humility toward one another
- fellowship with one another

The local church is the environment in which these activities should be occurring. These qualities are in contrast to how those in the world treat each other. Scripture speaks to this as well.

In the world we see people:

- consumed with passion toward one another
- passing judgment on one another
- filing lawsuits against one another
- depriving one another
- comparing themselves with one another
- biting and devouring one another

- provoking one another
- envying one another
- lying to one another
- hating one another
- speaking evil against one another
- grumbling against one another
- slaying one another

I don't know about you, but I'd rather experience the care that comes from those in the church. I've had more than enough experience in the world, where people are treated like garbage and it's every man for himself.

NO SOLO ARTISTS

The Christian who fails to interact with others in the context of the local church is missing out on part of God's plan for his or her life. Our towns are sprinkled with isolated Christians, and when I meet them and hear their reasons for dismissing the local church, I'm disgusted. I was recently in the home of one of these "solo artists" for Christ, and recognized that their minds had been poisoned against the local church. These people claimed to wholeheartedly love God (I don't doubt their sincerity), but they were in rebellion against His Word. You can't isolate yourself and be considered a true follower of Christ.

When a believer withdraws their family from fellowship, it's often a decision made out of fear. The husband and wife may have met in church, but when they had children they became afraid that their kids would be ruined by interacting with others and pulled them out of school and church. I would agree that in some cases the public school system is a less-than-ideal choice, but I have major issues with those who think that every local church is unsuitable for children and families.

It's true, churches sometimes have difficulty striking the balance between being inclusive and being protective. My wife and I were led by God to attend a particular church for a season, and I sensed that the youth group in that church was not an entirely safe environment for our teenage children. Some of the kids at the youth meetings didn't even attend the church, and it was obvious that some of the guys were just there to pursue the teenage girls. Having said that, the youth leaders and workers were people of strong character and were capable ministers.

My wife and I sought the Lord for His direction and concluded that it was okay for our children to participate in this youth group. However, He led us to be selective about which activities our children took part in, and we remained aware of who they were fellowshipping with. It ended up being a positive experience for our children. Had I allowed fear to influence my decision, completely restricting their involvement, my kids might have pulled back from serving God instead of drawing closer to Him. It's important to be led by the Spirit where your family's interests are concerned, understanding that God will never lead someone to completely separate from all others in the Body of Christ.

SELFISHNESS

> Loners who care only for themselves spit on the common good.
>
> Proverbs 18:1 (MSG)

I recently spoke with a neighbor who identified as a Christian. He mentioned that his wife really knew the Word and that his family prayed together every day. His next statement was one I've heard far too often. He said, "We're strong believers, we just don't do the church thing." Strong believers? In what? Not the book of Hebrews, the book of Acts, or the rest of the New Testament. They call themselves believers, but it would be more accurate to call them neglecters and forsakers.

I'm sure these folks never thought about it this way, but, by excusing themselves from the local church, they were committing a perpetual act of selfishness. They robbed others by not taking their rightful place of service within the

Body of Christ. Friends, *every* Christian can impact the lives of others. There's no impact, however, when we only focus on ourselves. You're not on Earth just for you. God has a work for you to accomplish as part of His Body. That work—without exception—will begin in the local church and will require interaction with others, both in the Body and not yet in the Body.

> For none of us lives to himself, and none of us dies
> to himself.
>
> Romans 14:7

ONE MAN'S MINISTRY

Many years ago, my wife and I visited the campus of the Bible school we were considering attending. There was a local church on that campus, and the day we were there happened to be the day of their regular midweek service. We were impressed with what we had seen so far at that ministry and were excited to visit the church. I'll never forget what happened on my way into the service.

There were two men standing by the doors, welcoming people as they entered the sanctuary. As I approached, one of these sharply dressed men took my hand, looked me in the eye, smiled and said, "Welcome to _____ Church."

You may think, "What's so unusual about that?" Nothing,

except that when he welcomed me, God's Spirit came upon me. I don't mean His power knocked me over, I just sensed an anointing that flowed as this man served in his area of ministry. This God-filled door-greeter was doing something that some might consider insignificant, but his ministry to me, another member of the Body, helped change the course of my life and solidified our decision to attend that school. It wasn't the music or the preaching that God used to minister to me the most that night; it was my brief interaction with a man I didn't even know (and still don't), who took his place of service within the Body of Christ.

Many underestimate the importance and power of ministering to one another. Others misinterpret what ministry to others means. Ministering to others doesn't always include counseling, prayer, or prophecy. I was ministered to by a greeting and a handshake. It seemed as though Jesus Himself was drawing me into the church through this man. That experience gave me the highest regard for what we call the "Ministry of Helps."

The strong believer is one whose life is intertwined with his or her local church. No believer can neglect their church and remain strong any more than an athlete can neglect diet and exercise and remain strong. Although the local church greatly benefits us, it's never *all* about us. God wants us at church for our own sake *and* for the sake of others that need ministry. As you focus on serving others, your needs will also be met. Your interaction, ministry, and fellowship with those around you will help sharpen and strengthen you.

Iron sharpens iron, and one man sharpens another.

Proverbs 27:17

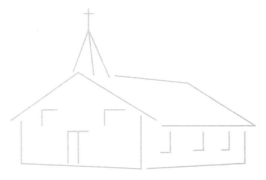

CHAPTER 8

More Meetings

Not neglecting to meet together, as is the habit of some, but encouraging one another, and **all the more** as you see the Day drawing near.

Hebrews 10:25

Racing is a past-time enjoyed throughout the world. Whether we're speaking of cars, horses, bicycles, skates, or man's two feet, there's a common element to all races: the participants must properly pace themselves throughout the race in order to finish strong. Sportscasters often comment that certain racers are using too much energy too soon and are in danger of not having enough "gas left in the tank" to finish their race.

Those who have paced themselves throughout a race put themselves in position to win at the end. Regardless of their starting position, skillful racers know how to make their move in the final lap. As the last corner is rounded, a great acceleration takes place, with all the racers sprinting toward the finish line.

The Church has been moving along the path of God's plan for centuries, and has rounded the corner into the last days. We can see the finish line where Christ will take us home. As they say in the world, it's time to "drive it like we stole it," hustling toward our goal while not allowing distractions to lead us off course. How does the Church properly accelerate in this last leg of our race? Hebrews 10:25 tells us: in order to finish strong, we must meet together *all the more.*

Okay, let's take this slowly to make sure we understand: the verse says *more*, not *less*, right? As we draw closer to the Return of the Lord, we should be meeting together for worship more and more. That means we should meet more often than in previous generations. Besides meeting regularly for worship, we must occasionally have special meetings and even some extended meetings.

I think you know where I'm headed with this. Right in the face of the command to meet together more and more, the Body of Christ has been meeting together less and less. Worshippers are staying home more often, so much so that some churches have been forced to close their doors. Once a week should evolve into two or three times a week but for many, once a week has turned into once a month. I sometimes feel as though the Church is barreling down a highway, but in the wrong direction. I want to get out in front of it and scream, "You're going the wrong way! Stop and turn around before you hit something!"

Attendance trends must mean nothing to us. People's busy schedules mean nothing. Hobbies, sports, and "must-see" TV shows definitely mean nothing. The command of God's Word is all that matters. The Word means everything. We disregard the low standards of society and hold to God's standard of righteousness. Just like we in Christ's Body won't redefine marriage to accommodate people's flesh, we won't redefine the place of the local church to accommodate fleshly desires. Whether society recognizes the meeting schedule of the local church, God still commands that we meet together often. We will not adjust to society, we only adjust to God.

NOAH'S EXAMPLE

> For as were the days of Noah, so will be the coming of the Son of Man.
>
> Matthew 24:37

The story of Noah wonderfully foreshadows the end-times. We see people who are stubborn, rebellious, and isolated being excluded from the plan of God. We see the patience of Noah as he spent decades preparing the ark that would bring God's creation safely into a new era. (Noah's ark is symbolic of the local church.) Then we see perhaps the most important part of this story: an unprecedented gathering together. A pair of each kind of animal supernaturally came together into the ark to journey to the other side of the flood. Although a terrible scene was unfolding outside the ark, inside there was peace and safety. The journey from ancient Earth to the post-flood era was simply not possible outside of the ark.

In our day—the days leading up to the Return of Christ—God is drawing people from every nation into their local churches to gather for worship. He is preparing them for a flood of His power and a great harvest of souls. As the animals were gathered together to reproduce and repopulate the Earth, believers in the local church are to spiritually reproduce themselves and populate Heaven. As in the days of Noah, our journey to a new era requires people to be in the ark. Thank God for our ark—the local church—our gathering place.

THE COMING OF THE LORD

It's interesting that the Coming of the Lord *(the Day drawing near)* is mentioned in connection with the meeting schedule of the local church. The reason we must meet together more often as we near His return is because our meetings affect His return. He is coming soon, but His coming does not just depend on the Father's will. The timing of His return is affected by the Church.

> Be patient, therefore, brothers, until the coming of the Lord. See how the farmer waits for the precious fruit of the earth, being patient about it, until it receives **the early and the late rains**.
>
> James 5:7

This verse shows why Christ has not yet returned for His Church. The farmer (our Father) is waiting for *the precious fruit of the earth*. Another scriptural term for the precious fruit of the earth is *the harvest* (a massive gathering of souls into the Kingdom of God). Christ will not return for the Church until the harvest has been reaped.

Reaping the harvest is the job of the Church. Preparing the workers to reap God's harvest is an important reason to meet together with increasing frequency. If the Church fails to meet, the reapers remain unprepared. If the reapers are asleep at the wheel, the harvest will not be reaped and Christ must continue to wait.

THE CHURCH AND THE RAIN

Notice that James speaks of *the early and the late rains.* Rain, in scripture, is symbolic of the moving and outpouring of the Spirit of God. No harvest can be reaped without sufficient rain. The outpouring of the rain of God's Spirit will cause His full harvest to be reaped. We would be correct in saying that Jesus cannot return for His Church until there's an intense, sustained outpouring of God's power upon the Earth.

What does this have to do with the local church? Everything. Those who understand how God works know that when He moves by His Spirit in the Earth, He does so through His Body, the Church. The Church receives the rain of God's Spirit and takes it to the world. This has been the pattern of every recorded outpouring on Earth, including the early rain of Acts chapter two. There, the disciples received the fullness of God's Spirit and took it to the world around them, reaping a great harvest.

If the Church will not meet together with increasing regularity, the outpouring of the Spirit will not be received and the Church will never learn to skillfully flow with God. As theologically awkward as this may sound, God is waiting for the Church to give Him the opportunity to move. If we're not meeting, God's not moving. If He's not moving, it's not raining. No rain, no harvest. No harvest, no return. I'm not saying that everything pertaining to Christ's return is up to us, but I believe that if the Church refuses to cooperate with God's plans, those plans will be delayed.

YOU'VE GONE AS FAR AS YOU CAN GO

When I pastored our church in New York, I endeavored to teach our people how to cooperate with the move of God. We would get to a certain place in the Spirit, but would only occasionally move further into a deeper flow. During a time of prayer, the Lord spoke to my heart and said, "This church has gone as far as it can go spiritually. There will be no further progress unless you start having some extended meetings." I knew what He meant, but was hesitant to move in that direction since I was still trying to train the people to come regularly on Sundays and Wednesdays.

As I sought Him further for His plan, He dealt with me about having two week-long meetings every year. This was in addition to our regular services, and the occasional two or three-day meetings we might have when a guest minister came to town. One of the week-long meetings would be conducted by myself, and the other would feature a team of ministers working together.

I began preparing our people for these meetings ahead of time, because I knew I was dealing with a culture where people are casual with their attendance. I told the people that it would be reasonable to expect substantial spiritual growth to occur in their lives during these weeks of meetings. Our people came expecting that, and they received accordingly. In just one week, our church progressed spiritually to a place we had never been before.

When I traveled with Brother Hagin, he was conducting meetings that were two weeks long (once, the meeting continued for a third week). In each meeting, about half-way through the second week, I would begin to notice how different I was on the inside. As the flow of God in the services increased, I would be carried to a higher place in God. Not only was my life blessed, those meetings equipped me to carry the same glorious atmosphere to others. There's no price too great to pay for daily being in God's presence and glory yet most people find it a burden to show up even once a week. Let's follow the example of the prophetess Anna, who made the house of God her place of continual refuge.

> She did not depart from the temple, worshiping with fasting and prayer night and day.
>
> Luke 2:37

I'm not satisfied with where we are in the Body of Christ. I'm ready to move on, and I know God is ready to move us on. There's a harvest to be reaped and an outpouring to be received. It starts as we align ourselves with His plan to come together more and more. Whether convenient or inconvenient, I'm all the way in and going all the way with Him. Will you join me?

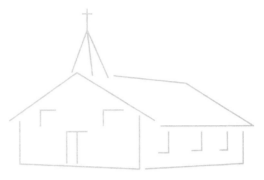

CHAPTER 9

A Place of Revelation

As time progresses, the local church is to have a greater place of importance and influence in the world. I realize that in many places the opposite has been true.

As the believer progresses through life, their knowledge and experience should cause them to place an increasingly higher value on the local church. Again, the opposite is too often true. I've known many people who started out in the local church but later left. Their stories are sad.

Although many do properly value the local church, others understand its place only in a limited measure, lacking the full revelation that God desires us to possess. The next several chapters will help us see the church as God sees it. Along the way, we'll explore reasons why the believer should allow nothing to keep him or her away from their local church and pastor.

REVELATION

The local church is one of the main avenues through which revelation from God flows. What do we mean by *revelation*? Revelation is the revealing of spiritual knowledge to the believer. Revelation is not the same as education (the receiving of intellectual knowledge). Revelation occurs as the Spirit of God takes the Word of God that is being preached and causes the meaning to explode within our hearts. Just as precious stones and minerals are hidden deep beneath the Earth's surface and must be mined, the Word of God is filled with nuggets of truth that must be spiritually uncovered.

Much of the revelation that enlightens the Christian is found in the pages of the New Testament letters, written by Paul and others. There's something significant about Paul's letters: every one of them was addressed either to a local church, a group of churches, or the pastor of a church. For example, Romans was written to the church in Rome. Galatians was written to a group of four churches in the region of Galatia. Titus was the pastor of the church at Crete, etc.

Why is this fact about Paul's letters so important? It shows that when God wants to reveal truth to the Body of Christ, He brings that truth to them through the local church.

Although the pages of scripture are no longer being penned, God still desires to reveal truth to man. He's not bringing revelation apart from the written Word, or in opposition to it, but is bringing revelation *from* His Word: truths embedded within Scripture that have not always been known or seen. There's always more to glean from Scripture, for no person has ever exhausted all the revelation that's in the Bible. As sure as you think you know it all, you'll realize that you hardly know anything at all. There's always more revelation because there's always more of God; He's infinite. Where would one go to receive this revelation from God today? We should expect revelation to come to us through the ministries of the local church, just as it has for centuries.

God certainly reveals truth to people as they study at home, watch Christian television, listen to recorded sermons, etc. However, the believer will never receive *all* the truth that he or she needs without faithfully attending their local church. Revelation flows to the believer as they are properly connected to their local church.

People who are rightly connected to the local church will glean more from their personal study time than the believer who's not in church. Having the right church and pastor will position a person to increase in spiritual knowledge. This is a wonderful thing. Remember, revelation is not received merely intellectually. Truth is imparted to the *spirit* of the believer before enlightening their mind. Things like disobedience or being out of one's place in the Body can keep a person from receiving from God, restricting the flow of revelation that God has for them.

Revelation can flow strongly during worship services, because worship creates an atmosphere ripe for the flow of God. You'll need to be in church to experience it. Much truth will come to the believer through their pastor, as he or she ministers the Word. We should expect revelation from God every time the church is open. You can't stay at home and receive these same things. Listening to a recording or watching online is good, but it's not as good as being present in an atmosphere of worship. It's always better to be there if possible.

The soccer field is not a place of revelation. Nature trails and lakes may inspire, but they aren't the place of revelation God has ordained. Malls, movie theaters, or concert or sports venues are not gathering places conducive to revelation. The local church is uniquely established as a place from which revelation from Heaven can flow. There's no place like the local church.

The person who's not in church needs one revelation above all: the revelation of the importance and place of the local church. A friend of mine likes to say, "God delivers your mail to your local church." Make sure you're there for mail call. It's not snail-mail or email; it's spirit-mail. Be there for it.

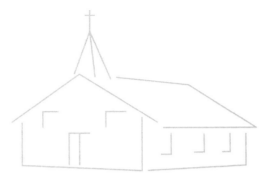

CHAPTER 10

Correction and Direction

The local church is a place where the believer can receive correction, direction, and leading. It's where we go to hear from God—a place of safe counsel—a place of answers.

I've been in restaurants where groups of ladies (or men) were meeting together, and I could hear as one began sharing with the others about their marriage problems. Those at the table were sympathetic to their troubled friend and joined in condemning the non-present spouse. Although counsel was freely flowing at the table, most of the counsel I've heard in restaurants should never have been offered.

Go to church to get things straightened out, not the

restaurant. There's more help for you at church than there is at the restaurant or coffee shop. It's amazing where people turn (and where they don't turn) when they need help. Some actually leave their local church and pastor during times of trouble instead of recognizing it as their place of help and safety.

Over the years, we had a handful of people at our church with marriage problems. Of those, I can't recall even one couple who came to us for help during their time of difficulty. They would keep their troubles a secret and then vanish from church right before getting a divorce. I would think that admitting there's a problem and asking for help early on would be an easier path to follow than going through a divorce. It almost seemed as if people would rather divorce than admit to their pastor that they need help. Here's a newsflash for you: your pastor already knows you need help. We all need help.

I haven't done everything perfectly in life and I've missed it at times. I *know* I need help! There are places I go and people I turn to for correction and help. I'm not just speaking of private counsel; I rarely ask for that (although I would if I needed to). I'm speaking of going to certain places to get under the anointing that brings guidance, direction, and help to my life. That same anointing is available for you at your local church. Be present in church while your pastor is under the anointing and expect God to deliver your answer as he or she ministers. That's a great way to get the counsel you need.

I was once listening to a preacher who, in his younger years, had lived with Brother Hagin. Although he had a level of access to this great man that most others did not, he learned it was best not to ask question after question while in his home. He said, "When I had a question I knew Brother Hagin could answer, I learned to instead ask God that question. Then, I would pay close attention in the services where Brother Hagin was ministering and would invariably receive my answer." That advice has helped me receive from great men and women of God over the years.

HOW JESUS BROUGHT CORRECTION

Pastors must at times bring correction to their congregations just like Jesus, the Chief Shepherd, brings correction to His Body. How does Jesus do that? He corrects His Body through the ministry of the local church.

While in exile on the island of Patmos, the Apostle John had an experience where Jesus appeared to him, showing him many things that would come to pass in the future. Prior to revealing those things, Jesus took time to bring correction and direction to His Body, the Church.

While speaking with John in this vision, Jesus dictated

letters to the seven churches of Asia Minor. These churches were literal local congregations in actual cities. In these letters, Jesus commended the churches for things that they were doing well, but also brought correction in areas where they were falling short (it can be easy for a ministry or church to veer off course without realizing it). Thank God, He loves us enough to bring correction when needed. We too should expect to receive correction for our lives in our local church.

As one of the few remaining original apostles, John had a ministry to the entire Body of Christ. Jesus could have led him to minister these things to the Body in a general fashion, but He instead brought correction to these churches individually. I believe He did this to emphasize the importance of the local church, establishing it as a place where believers may receive direction and guidance.

Each of these seven letters that Jesus dictated in Revelation concluded with this phrase: *He who has an ear, let him hear what the Spirit says to the churches.* Repetition in Scripture is significant, so it's worth noting that this phrase is repeated seven different times. This indicates that, just as Christ brought correction to the churches on this occasion, the Spirit would do the same going forward. Notice that Jesus didn't say, "Let him hear what the Spirit says to *the Church*." He emphasized *churches*: local congregations. God, by His Spirit, continues to direct and correct congregations today. The local church, under the leadership of the pastor, is our place of correction and direction.

CORRECTION IN THE CHURCH

> To learn, you must love discipline; it is stupid to hate correction.
>
> Proverbs 12:1 (NLT)

One reason people reject their place in the local church is that they're not open to godly correction. Many in our day so despise correction that a new type of church has emerged to accommodate them: one that only preaches a positive, feel-good message (never anything corrective). People who attend such churches are, in some respects, wasting their time. A believer will never grow, mature, or make progress without correction.

To reject correction is to reject one of the primary purposes of God's Word. Notice what Paul wrote to Timothy, a young pastor:

> Every part of Scripture is God–breathed and useful one way or another--showing us truth, exposing our rebellion, correcting our mistakes, training us to live God's way.
>
> 2 Timothy 3:16 (MSG)

Each of the above purposes of God's Word can be corrective, requiring the believer to make adjustments and changes to his or her life. While there's plenty of truth in the Word of God that's inspiring and motivational, if we only focus on things that "feel good" we'll have little use for much of the Word (which is why some ministers, sadly, rarely use the Bible in their preaching and teaching). No, we need *all* of the Word. As the verse above teaches, *every* part of the Word is useful and good. We must consider correction, rebuke, and training to be good things, and adopt a philosophy that says, "If it's good for me, I want it."

I want correction. I want to know where I'm missing it (if I am missing it). I need the truth, even if it's sometimes hard to hear. Christians shouldn't get upset when their pastor preaches corrective truth. They should thirst for correction. "Pastor, please show me what's right!" should be the cry of the believer who possesses a teachable spirit. Correction is a friend to the Christian, not an enemy.

MINISTERING CORRECTION

While the believer must remain open to correction, leaders must be careful to minister it correctly, with proper motives and a right spirit. For example, in most cases, ministers are not to address the specific personal issues of their congregants from the pulpit. They're not to "take shots" at people from the pulpit, forcing correction upon those who need it. The preacher is simply to preach the Word of God as he or she is led by God. Such ministry will bring correction to the hearers in a way that can best be received. Will everyone receive God's correction? Regrettably, no. If a person chooses not to receive the correction that the Word offers, he or she is free to reject it.

> You ignored my advice and rejected the correction I offered.
>
> Proverbs 1:25 (NLT)

Ministers are never to manipulate people, trying to force them to obey God. Manipulation and forcefulness are trademarks of the devil, not God. God leads with love. Satan forces and coerces. To force a person to do anything (even trying to force their obedience to God) resembles the work of the enemy more than the ministry of the Lord. Like all ministers, I've had to come to terms with the fact that I won't be able to help everyone. Not every person will bear fruit, and many won't even stay around long enough to give the things of God the opportunity to work in their lives. We must simply go on and help those who will receive their help.

While we don't condone manipulation, we must still bring godly correction at times. Not everyone understands the difference between the two.

A ministry leader I know once took a survey based on a statement he had heard. He said, "I hear some ministers are telling people that if they leave their church, bad things will happen to them." This leader then allowed his readers to comment on that statement. As I read dozens of comments from the respondents (most of whom were in ministry), I was a bit surprised.

Almost every response condemned that statement as an act of manipulation. Few saw it as an act of love and godly correction. (Of course, without knowing the context, it's impossible to tell whether such a statement was manipulative or if it was a loving warning.) When I read that statement, I thought, *Maybe there's a better way to say it, but that's basically true. If you leave the place in which God has planted you, there's no doubt things won't go well.* No person has ever jumped out of the will of God without eventually experiencing negative consequences.

I've encouraged some who were leaving my church to rethink their decision, considering the possible negative outcomes. I warned them out of love and concern for them, not because I was trying to coerce them into staying (I actually don't desire people to remain in my congregation who resent being there). It's not that their departure would hurt me, but their decision to leave over an offense would negatively affect them and the other members of their family. I don't enjoy confrontation and would always rather not say anything, but the love of God in me will lead me to speak up at times.

The job of the minister is to share truth with people, publicly from the pulpit, and privately as God leads. If the minister obeys God, speaking what He says the way He says it, he's done his part and must leave the results with God. Although I've endeavored to be led of the Spirit and speak as God directed, I've nevertheless had people accuse me of acting like a mafia boss. They told others that I threatened them when I suggested they prayerfully consider the move they were about to make. I threatened no one, but lovingly shared the principles of God's Word. Once they followed through with their decision, I didn't try to get them to change their mind.

SHEPHERDSHIP

We must remain balanced in this area of correction and guidance. I was around for the Shepherdship Movement in the 1980s (also known as the Discipleship Movement) and saw firsthand the pitfalls of extreme leadership. I had friends who were required to submit every personal decision to the leadership of their church. I've known of pastors who selected spouses for their members (those marriages didn't last). They told their people where to invest their money (that didn't work out either), what jobs to take, and what kind of car to buy. Those who didn't obey were intimidated and ostracized. Many of my friends from that time, attempting to escape the control of their spiritual leaders, stopped serving God altogether. Extreme correction and guidance like the examples I just shared creep into the church every so often, but that in no way resembles the kind of scriptural help I'm referring to.

Most people today are far from the errors of the Shepherdship Movement, but many have gone so far in the other direction that they're in the ditch on the other side of the road. Today's concept of the local church often includes no accountability at all. People's level of involvement and commitment is shallow. Many are disconnected from their local church, unable to take advantage of the great help God has made available to them. Just as we reject the ditch of extreme leadership, we must reject the ditch of loose local church affiliation. Let's swing back into the middle of the road where commitment and accountability are found.

THE ADVANTAGE

> Obey your leaders and submit to them, for they are keeping watch over your souls, as those who will have to give an account. Let them do this with joy and not with groaning, for that would be of no advantage to you.
>
> Hebrews 13:17

This verse ends with the phrase *advantage to you*. Obedience and submission are not just for the benefit of the leader, they bless your life, bringing you an advantage. I don't know about you, I'll take any advantage I can get. You don't even need to be a believer to understand the value of having an advantage. Some parents begin training their children in sports such as gymnastics and figure skating when they're barely old enough to walk. They want them to have a head start: an advantage over the competition. All the Christian need do to have the advantage is obey and submit to those over them (including the Holy Spirit within them). Submission and obedience don't hold people back, they propel them forward. They don't bring bondage, they bring blessing and freedom.

Who are the leaders in this verse to whom we must submit? It can only be speaking of the pastor of the local church. Civic leaders must also be obeyed, but they don't keep watch over your soul. Your pastor is the one who does that. Other leaders are important, but they won't give an account to God for your life. The pastor has that responsibility, and it will be to your advantage if he can joyfully recount his time with you.

The primary way a person obeys his or her pastor is by being a doer of the Word the pastor preaches. Indeed, the best way to honor your man or woman of God is to do what they say. Put into practice the principles that he or she teaches.

Obedience to a ministry leader doesn't mean that he or she exercises control over your life. Pastors have enough decisions to make in their own lives and ministries. They don't need, nor should they desire, the task of making other people's decisions for them.

The Word your pastor preaches brings direction to your life. Follow that direction and you'll enjoy success. Rebel against it and you'll forfeit success. That's not a threat, it's the truth! When making major decisions in life, take advantage of the wisdom that's in your pastor. That wisdom is part of the anointing upon his or her life. If your pastor is younger than you, don't think he or she can't be a help. God has anointed him or her to speak into your life.

ASK YOUR PASTOR

If you're considering a serious relationship with someone, it's wise to seek the counsel of your pastor (in a larger church, there may be others on staff whom the pastor has appointed to assist). Ask his or her opinion and be willing to hear whatever he or she has to say. Never make decisions based on feelings or emotions. It's best to speak with your pastor about these types of things early in a relationship, before you fall in love (it's possible to fall in love with someone and God not be in it at all). Your pastor is a neutral party and can assess the situation with clarity. If you're moving in an opposing direction to the will of God, your pastor (with God's help) can sense it and will advise you, saving you headache and heartache.

If you or a family member are facing a major medical decision, talk to your pastor. He or she has spent many years learning how to hear from God, and can provide comfort and confirmation by coming alongside you in prayer. It's not the pastor's job to decide for you or tell you what to do, but he or she can nevertheless bring a precious degree of help to your life. Pastors want nothing more than to see their people enjoying success and experiencing God's best. Be willing to receive God's loving correction and you'll always be able to receive His guidance and direction.

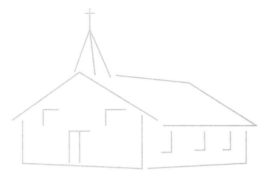

CHAPTER 11

Development and Growth

> And he gave the apostles, the prophets, the evangelists, the shepherds and teachers, to equip the saints for the work of ministry, for building up the body of Christ, until we all attain to the unity of the faith and of the knowledge of the Son of God, to mature manhood, to the measure of the stature of the fullness of Christ.
>
> Ephesians 4:11-13

This verse teaches that the local church is a place of development and growth. That means Christians attend church to grow and change rather than to remain the same. If someone asks why you're always at church, tell them, "I go to grow." Without church, the Christian remains in a babyhood state—undeveloped in faith—deficient in spiritual understanding. The believer who fails to grow cannot fulfill the place of ministry that God has for him or her.

To help the Christian grow, God has placed ministry offices in the Body of Christ. Where does one go to receive from the apostle, prophet, evangelist, pastor, and teacher? More than any other place, they're found functioning in the local church. Without regular exposure to these ministries, the believer cannot progress to spiritual adulthood.

The believer receives from their pastor more frequently than any of the other offices. For that reason, the pastor's office should be considered the most essential. Connecting to one's pastor and learning the different ways his ministry operates is where it all starts for the believer. The other ministry offices come alongside to support, enhance, and compliment the pastor's office and fortify the local church. God may greatly use the ministries of others who are not pastors, but every ministry has the responsibility of emphasizing the importance and place of the local church.

PUTTING THE LOCAL CHURCH FIRST

Over the years, I've seen traveling or television ministers

disregard the place of the local church. That's an error. Many desire to promote their own ministry, but non-church ministries should never act as a substitute for the local church. Some of these ministers ask for and receive tithes from their followers. That's improper and harmful to the local church. Ministers ought not emphasize their ministry in a way that leads people to discount their local church and pastor. Ministers who do so are missing the emphasis of God's Word.

The Apostle Paul is an example of a minister who, although not a pastor, continually emphasized the place of the local church. There were times when Paul received less compensation than was due him in order to avoid overburdening the growing churches to whom he was ministering. If he was like some ministers in our day, he would have promoted partnership with his ministry at the exclusion of the local church. Although he did encourage people to sow into his ministry, he did so in a balanced fashion. Thank God for Paul's example.

My spiritual father, Rev. Kenneth E. Hagin, is another example of a minister who always directed people to their own local church and pastor. Because of his well-placed priorities, he received a great harvest of growth in his own ministry. While many other ministries may be worthy of our attention and support, we must remain established in the fact that it's all about the local church.

There are some things—counseling, for example—that

the believer should primarily receive through the ministry of their local church. Their pastor may refer them for help outside the church, but it's important that the believer go to their pastor first. Don't just call some other ministry's prayer hotline. Don't just run to your neighborhood counseling center. Go where God's anointing is. Go to your pastor! Don't fall into the trap of believing that you know more than your pastor, or presume that he or she is not qualified to help you. Your pastor is anointed to speak into your life in a way other counselors or therapists are not.

We must keep these things in order. Please don't think I'm against other types of ministries or believe that all but the pastor are unimportant. I recognize that four of the five ministries listed in our text in Ephesians four are non-pastoral, yet essential. My own ministry doesn't include the pastoral office. My point is, all ministers and ministries must direct people to the local church, being careful to put it first.

NO CHURCH, NO GROWTH

> The righteous shall flourish like the palm tree: he shall grow like a cedar in Lebanon. **Those that be planted in the house of the Lord shall flourish** in the courts of our God. They shall still bring forth fruit in old age; they shall be fat and flourishing.
>
> Psalms 92:12-14

When I was first saved, it was quite an adventure. Having been raised Jewish, I knew nothing about local churches other than that they existed. My few Christian friends, regrettably, didn't emphasize to me the importance of the local church (I'm not sure they were in church themselves). Soon after I was saved however, one of my friends started a Bible study group at the place of business where we all worked.

Having just given my heart to the Lord, I was excited to attend. Since they called it a Bible study, I figured I had better purchase a Bible (we didn't have any Bibles lying around our Jewish home). My friend brought me to a place called a "Christian Bookstore" where I could purchase one. I'll never forget purchasing that first Bible. It looked so nice and even smelled nice. I kept reading the table of contents; there were a lot of books in the Bible!

For two years I attended that Bible study on Thursday nights. We enjoyed each other's fellowship, and I learned many things about the Word of God. The teacher of our Bible study had been part of a church, but that church had been going through a season of difficulty, having just parted ways with a pastor whose leadership had been divisive. When it was announced that a former pastor of that church would be returning, my friend suggested we discontinue our study group and instead all go to church together. Smart decision.

Two years after having been saved, I began attending church and, for the first time, began to grow spiritually.

Looking back, I see that while I attained knowledge of the things of God in my friend's Bible study, my inner man had never grown and developed. I find it significant that the moment I became connected to my local church and pastor, I began to grow spiritually. I had been missing the pastor's office and anointing in my life and, of course, didn't even know it.

The Bible says *knowledge puffs up* (1 Corinthians 8:1). When something is puffed up, it looks like true growth but is really not. It's just inflated. The kind of knowledge that puffs up is not revelation knowledge but intellectual knowledge. Although my newfound knowledge of the Bible made it look like I was growing, I was not truly developing spiritually. As I've said, not all growth is good growth. A tumor is growth in the human body, but it's not the right kind of growth. We don't want false growth, we only want real spiritual growth.

Everything about that local church seemed to help me develop spiritually. As I sat under my pastor's ministry, I was being spiritually fed. My fellowship with the other members of the church helped me develop. Worshipping with the congregation helped me recognize the presence of God. I grew as I attended my Sunday School class.

Here's an interesting fact: my Sunday School teacher was the same person who taught our Bible study during the first two years of my Christian life. I was under the same teaching, but this time it was rightly submitted under the authority of the pastor. Because that class was part of the local church, both my teacher (as a minister) and I (as a student) were partaking of the pastor's anointing, even though the pastor wasn't present in the classroom. What was the result? I grew.

Can you see how different everything is when connected to the local church? The local church is the chief place that God has ordained for ministry. I'm not a big fan of home groups, Bible studies, prayer groups, etc. that aren't under the authority of the local church, because I know it's so easy to substitute these things for the local church. I can tell you from experience, it's easier on the flesh to be part of a home group than a church. No spiritual authority, no tithing, no Ministry of Helps, etc. There's also no pastoral anointing, which is the element that allows spiritual growth to occur. Get in church and then participate in any groups you like that your church sponsors.

KEEPERS OF THE MYSTERIES

Take care not to minimize the importance of your church. It's your place of feeding: your spiritual supply. If you see your church correctly, you'll protect and care for it. One way you care for it is by being a good steward of the truths you're receiving. Another way you care for it is by serving. Service and stewardship will occupy the believer who views their local church correctly. Notice this great statement from the

Apostle Paul:

> This is how one should regard us, as servants of Christ and stewards of the mysteries of God. Moreover, it is required of stewards that they be found faithful.
>
> 1 Corinthians 4:1-2

What does it mean to be *stewards of the mysteries of God?* A steward is a manager, guard, or keeper. The phrase *mysteries of God* refers to revelation from God's Word (before you received truth from God's Word, it was all a mystery to you). When a person guards the revelation they've received, they're being good stewards of those truths. They are *stewards of the mysteries of God.* We should think of ourselves as *mystery managers:* caring for the revelation we've received and putting God's Word into practice in our lives. Many other verses similarly speak about guarding the truths we've received. Here's one of the most powerful:

> Therefore we must pay much closer attention to what we have heard, lest we drift away from it.
>
> Hebrews 2:1

There are some practical ways by which we can exercise good stewardship. First, always bring your Bible to church. Even if the scriptures are being displayed or projected, it will help you to turn in your own Bible and underline, highlight, or make notes on the things that the Lord is impressing upon you.

Taking notes during the service is a great way to retain what is being taught and preached. I have notebooks full of revelation from services I have attended, and every so often will go back and review those notes. When I do, the revelation becomes fresh to me again. Jot down the scripture references the pastor uses in his messages so you can review them later. The sermon itself (no matter how good) is not what's most important. It's the *truth* in the sermon that will most minister to you, and that truth must be reviewed and studied if it's to become part of your life. Be a good steward and a good student of the truth you've received.

DISQUALIFIED

We had people in our church whose lives were completely changed by the things of God. Some were saved in our church. Others were filled with the Spirit or healed there. Many spent years under our teaching and experienced great growth. Some, however, would grow to a certain point but then refuse to progress to full maturity.

One such lady had attended our church for years. She had grown spiritually, served in the Ministry of Helps, and was a delight to be around. However, she would always back off from flowing with God when the Spirit began to move in a service. It seemed like the deeper the move, the more she dug her heels in resistance. As time went on, I could tell that her resistance in this one area was causing her not to receive from God like she previously had. When we refuse to walk in the light God has given us, we close ourselves to further light.

I was surprised one day to receive a *Dear Pastor* letter from her in the mail. (A Dear Pastor letter is the local church equivalent of a Dear John letter, when a lady writes to break up with a man, saying she's found someone else. Every pastor has probably received these types of letters or emails). This lady thanked us for leading her to Christ and raising her in the things of God, but informed us she would be attending another church from then on. The church she mentioned was one that barely preached the new birth, much less the deeper things of God. I knew she would never get spiritually fed there.

I started to pray about this situation, endeavoring to discern whether the Lord would have me respond to her letter. As I prayed, the Lord spoke to me. He said, "Let her go. She's disqualified herself from her place of feeding." When He said that I thought, "Can you do that?" Evidently you can or He wouldn't have said it. Many have disqualified themselves from their place of feeding by not being good stewards of the revelation they had received, and by refusing to walk on into greater light.

I wish I could say this lady was the only person to have ever been disqualified from participation in our ministry; however, I suspect that's not the case. Since the Lord spoke that phrase to me, I've recognized it as the reason some others may have departed. It's possible for an entire church to disqualify themselves from the pastor that God gave them by failing to care for, support, and receive from that pastor. This kind of thing happens all the time. Even the Apostle Paul had people who deserted him, having failed to recognize and esteem their God-ordained connection to his ministry. One such person was a man named Demas. I wonder if Demas had any idea at all who (and what) he was leaving.

> For Demas hath forsaken me, having loved this present world, and is departed unto Thessalonica; Crescens to Galatia, Titus unto Dalmatia.
>
> 2 Timothy 4:10 (KJV)

Let's recognize our place of feeding, understanding the responsibilities that are attached to that place, and let's be good stewards of the mysteries of God. Your place of growth, development, and feeding is your local church. Your stewardship and servanthood in your church will produce a lasting harvest of blessing and reward.

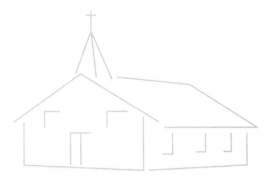

Chapter 12

Safety and Protection

I enjoy secret-agent-type action movies. Usually, the good guys are walking the line between life and death during the entire course of the movie, living on the edge to protect the world from annihilation. I like the thrill of the chase and find myself sympathizing with the agents who just want the bad guy to go away or die so they can relax and have a little breathing room.

Often, the agency that employs these super-agents has set up secret places in major cities throughout the world to which their agents can retreat. These places are called safe-houses. When the action gets too heavy, you'll find everyone regrouping at the safe-house.

For the believer, the local church is their safe-house into which they can perpetually run. The church should be safe in every respect, for there are few truly safe places in the world. It's the pastor's responsibility to keep the church safe by protecting the sheep and keeping out the wolves. There are even times when it may be necessary for the pastor to remove a person from fellowship for the protection of the rest of the sheep.

The pastor doesn't just function on a natural level as chief security guard of the church. He also works as a secret agent in the spirit realm, helping make the local church a place of safety and protection.

SPIRITUAL PROTECTION

> Obey your leaders and submit to them, for they are **keeping watch over your souls,** as those who will have to give an account. Let them do this with joy and not with groaning, for that would be of no advantage to you.
>
> Hebrews 13:17

The absence of predators (as wonderful as that is) is not the main reason the church is a safe-house. The church is a safe place because of the anointing. As shown in the text above, the pastor is charged with keeping watch over the believers in his care. He's able to do this for his flock, no matter how large, by his pastoral anointing.

What does this watchfulness look like, practically speaking? It can mean that if a church member (or their family) is headed for a dangerous or difficult situation, the pastor will know it by the Spirit and can deal with it. He may know it by the word of knowledge, or may just have a general burden to pray without knowing what or whom he's praying for. Either way, the problem can be dealt with. This kind of supernatural help and protection belongs to all of God's children, but is only experienced by those who are connected to their local church.

The person who only occasionally attends church is not allowing their pastor to sufficiently keep watch over them because they are not keeping themselves under his anointing. If your pastor rarely sees you, he can't keep watch over you. During the several years that I pastored, I discovered that the people I could help the most were ones who were the most closely connected to the church.

On one occasion, a key leader in our church suffered a life-threatening emergency. When I reached the hospital, I was able to look him in the eye and tell him he was going to be all right. I knew that if he wasn't going to make it, or if additional complications were imminent, God would have told me. I knew this in my spirit as an absolute certainty. All turned out just as we knew it would. That leader later testified how comforting and precious our ministry to him was at that time. What I said to him in that hospital room was not something I could have said to every member of our congregation, because not all were connected well enough for me to effectively keep watch over them.

How do you know if you're properly connected with your church and pastor? Here's one good test: if you don't know the name of your church or the pastor's full name, you're not well connected. I meet people all the time who tell me they go to church but can't even tell me the church's name. Usually they're not lying, because when they describe the church, I can tell them the name and the pastor's name, and a look of recognition flashes across their face as they exclaim, "Yeah, that's it." If what I just described rings true for you, it's time to make some changes. Get closer, get involved, and get blessed.

I want my spiritual life to be such that those over me can easily watch over my soul. That doesn't mean I have to be close with my leaders on a personal level. In a larger church, you could be rightly connected without the pastor even knowing your name. You simply need to be there—all the time—taking your place of service. When the pastor and congregation members alike yield to God in obedience, a great level of care and protection is available.

JOY OR GROANING?

Our text in Hebrews 13:17 indicates that leaders will have to give account to God regarding those entrusted to their care. The following phrase says *let them do this with joy and not with groaning.* Although I've not yet stood before the judgement seat of Christ, I've still groaned about way too many people in my years of ministry. I much prefer being able to answer with joy.

On a recent trip to the town in which I formerly pastored, I ran into a relative of one of my former members. This church member had pulled their family out of our church after many years (I never knew the reason), and I knew how their departure would affect the children in the family. Those children had been raised in our church. When children are suddenly separated from the only pastor they've ever known, it's a much more traumatic experience than the parents realize.

Our role as pastors brought a degree of protection to those children, including providing a measure of godly restraint to their lives. That restraining influence was removed when the parents took the children out from under our spiritual care. I asked this relative how these children were doing, and we both had what I would call a *groan-fest*. One of the kids had a child out of wedlock and was moving around from man to man. The other was dealing with substance abuse and was quite rebellious. Groan, groan, groan. They turned out just as I had seen years before. It's so much better to be able to answer with joy instead of groaning.

SAFE IN THE LOCAL CHURCH

When an individual is part of a local church, he or she will also be watched over by the other members of that church community. We've already observed how the Bible emphasizes each believer's care for one another. In my church, I didn't have to provide a lot of pastoral care. The love of God shown by our members toward others in our church family was so outstanding that my personal involvement was not always necessary.

People were always calling, bringing meals, praying for, and encouraging one other. There was one couple in our church who were so committed to interacting with visitors and new families that I never had to formally organize any kind of follow-up program. There was a flow of follow-up and care in our church because our people had learned how to put the love of God into action. Every believer should be a part of such a community.

If someone who regularly attended our church was missing one week, someone close to them would check in to make sure they were okay. There were occasions where a member of the church was unwell and could have died had a fellow member not checked in with them. The local church can be a life saver!

On the other hand, when a person is sporadic in their attendance, never involving themselves in the work of the ministry, it's difficult for them to benefit from the protection available within the local church. How would we know to check in on an occasional attender who is missing? I've had such people show up to a service and angrily exclaim, "I almost died a few weeks ago, and no one from this church called me." We didn't know they were sick. They never called to tell us, and were never involved enough to establish much of a spiritual connection. If loose attendance habits are keeping your pastor in the dark, make some lifestyle changes right away. It's dangerous to live apart from the protective care of your pastor. The best way to stay safe is to stay close to the local church.

EASY PREY

> Like a bird that wanders from its nest is a man who wanders from his place.
>
> Proverbs 27:8

Animals graze and travel together in herds for one main reason: protection against predators. The animal off by itself is easily picked off: a walking advertisement that dinner is served. Likewise, the Christian off by him or herself is easy prey for the enemy. It's unsafe for the Christian to be alone. The isolated Christian lacks sufficient protection against the enemy's schemes. Regardless of how many scriptures they can quote or how much they pray, a Christian apart from his or her safe-house is headed for trouble.

Many in the Body of Christ misjudge the importance of the local church. Some have learned to "put on the armor of God" and think that alone protects them from the enemy's schemes. No, they're safe only if they also obey other areas of the Word such as walking in love, speaking right words, and giving the local church its rightful place. We must avoid practicing only those parts of the Word that we like while neglecting parts we don't like.

Many believers practice selective obedience. I call them *Cafeteria Christians*: those who pick and choose areas of obedience the way a person would choose their meal in a cafeteria. They allow personal preference and convenience to guide their obedience instead of God's Word. They don't realize that their disobedience toward certain parts of the Bible negates the effectiveness of their obedience to other parts. Don't be like the bird that wanders from its nest. Satan would love nothing better than to get the believer off by him or herself where he can beat the stuffing out of them.

I often hear of situations in the lives of Christians I know that sadden me. Some of these are fellow ministers who suffer great difficulty or even tragedy. While some would ask, "How could this happen?" my first question is, "Where does this family attend church?" So often the answer is, "Nowhere." Some think that their ministries exempt them from participation in the local church. Although they may be out on the road ministering in churches, their families need a home church and pastor. All must learn that the Word we preach to others also applies to us.

I don't want my family (or myself) to be easy prey for the enemy, so we stay as close as possible to the local church: our safe-house. Let's be people who abide in our place of safety. No leader will have to groan about the Christian who is established in his or her place of feeding. Thank God for the local church: our place of safety and protection.

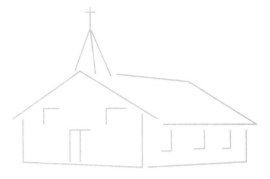

CHAPTER 13

Power and Visitation

So I have looked upon you in the sanctuary, behold-
ing your power and glory.

Psalms 63:2

When God's power moves on the Earth, it flows pre-
cisely, not randomly. A suitable place for that power
must be prepared, just as we make preparation for natural
power.

We call natural power *electricity*. For electricity to benefit our lives, it must be harnessed according to natural law,

which dictates where and how it can flow.

We don't place a floor lamp outside in a lightning storm hoping that it will receive power, nor do we just throw prayers toward Heaven, hoping for a release of spiritual power. For God's power to bless our lives, we must cooperate with it according to the principles set forth in scripture— spiritual law. His power flows the strongest when a place has been prepared for it according to spiritual law.

To put high-voltage power into a form that can safely power our homes and businesses, the electric company routes it through localized substations where it's then distributed throughout the neighborhood. God also routes His power through substations so it can be delivered to the lives of the people who need it. These substations are local churches: God's power distribution centers. Notice how the Church, at its inception, became a place of power:

> When the day of Pentecost arrived, they were all together in one place. And suddenly there came from heaven a sound like a mighty rushing wind, and it filled the entire house where they were sitting. And divided tongues as of fire appeared to them and rested on each one of them. And they were all filled with the Holy Spirit and began to speak in other tongues as the Spirit gave them utterance.
>
> Acts 2:1-4

The sound of Heaven's power penetrating the Earth on the Day of Pentecost is something I would have very much liked to hear. I've heard natural power make some interesting sounds during storms, with transformers humming and popping. I don't think anything in the natural could compare with that sound from Heaven, however. The sound of the entrance of God's power created quite a stir.

> Now there were dwelling in Jerusalem Jews, devout men from every nation under heaven. And at this sound the multitude came together, and they were bewildered, because each one was hearing them speak in his own language.
>
> Acts 2:5-6

God knows how to make sounds that attract the multitudes. People gather in the same way today when they hear of God's power in manifestation. We need displays and demonstrations of God's power that will draw the attention of those in the world who are not normally conscious of the things of God.

Notice the environment in which God's power could be received. They were *all together in one place*. That phrase is significant. God's power could not have flowed like it did had the disciples not been meeting together. They weren't at home watching the service online (I realize such technology didn't exist back then); they weren't missing half their people; they were all together in one place. An earlier passage in Acts suggests they had been meeting together for several days:

> All these with one accord were devoting themselves to prayer, together with the women and Mary the mother of Jesus, and his brothers. In those days Peter stood up among the brothers (the company of persons was in all about 120) and said. . . .
>
> Acts 1:14-15

The Day of Pentecost came ten days after the ascension of Jesus. It's safe to assume that the disciples had been meeting together at least daily for that week-and-a-half, engaged in spiritual activity in an atmosphere of unity. This type of gathering reveals a pattern that can be duplicated by others who are hungry to accommodate the power of God. Like the early disciples, we must meet together in unity, sometimes for extended seasons. The local church is the place where believers in our day meet together. Like the upper room on the Day of Pentecost, it's an appropriate landing place for the power of God.

God's power can (and does) flow in places other than the

local church (just like electricity is found in many places), however, the strongest flow of God's power will usually be within the local church. The local church is the gathering place for people of faith, and His power flows wherever faith is active. Healing power can be ministered anywhere, but should flow strongly in the local church. God's power to deliver works anywhere, but should be most easily accessed in the local church.

THE LAST DAYS MOVE OF GOD

Those who have had a major prophetic voice on the Earth have spoken of an end-time revival that will be based in the local church. Although the church might seem like an obvious location, many past revivals have taken place outside the church. When pastors, leaders, or congregations reject the flow of God, God is forced to bypass the local church and send His power elsewhere. The Last Day's Revival, however, *must* be in the local church, because the local church is the only place suitable to receive the level of power needed to bring us to the end of the age.

This revival won't be confined to the local church—it will simply be headquartered there. The power of God proceeds from the local church and flows out to a needy world. Believers who are full of faith, the Holy Spirit, and power are the ones who are to carry God's power and love to the dying world around them. Every Christian should think of him or herself as a storage battery for God's power, and should think of the local church as the charging or filling station where they plug in and charge up.

A FLOW OF POWER

> Afterward he brought me again unto the door of **the house**; and, behold, **waters issued out from under the threshold of the house** eastward: for the forefront of the house stood toward the east, and the waters came down from under from the right side of the house, at the south side of the altar.
>
> Ezekiel 47:1 (KJV)

The house in this passage is a reference to God's Temple. The Old Testament temple is symbolic of the Spirit-indwelled Body of Christ today. The temple is also symbolic of the local church, referred to in the New Testament as *the house of God* (1 Timothy 3:15). Water, as seen in this verse, represents the moving of the Spirit of God and the flow of His power.

The symbolic language used in this passage clearly shows power flowing from the house of God: the local church. That power is not confined to the house of God, but flows out to affect the world. Later verses in this chapter help us see that as God's power flows, it increases in intensity, rising above the river banks, catching many in its current, and changing the surrounding landscape. We need such change in our day, but it's only brought about by the power of God.

> Going on eastward with a measuring line in his hand, the man measured a thousand cubits, and then led me through the water, and it was ankle-deep. Again he measured a thousand, and led me through the water, and it was knee-deep. Again he measured a thousand, and led me through the water, and it was waist-deep. Again he measured a thousand, and it was a river that I could not pass through, for the water had risen. It was deep enough to swim in, a river that could not be passed through.
>
> Ezekiel 47:3-5

This power is available all the time, but until the Church learns to cooperate with it, we won't see it flowing as we ought. We develop skill with God's power by coming together in His presence where His power manifests. This is another reason not to neglect meeting together for worship. We could think of every service as a practice session, where we gain more experience cooperating with God's power.

Let's not be satisfied with less than God's best in this area. I don't know about you, but I tire of people being thrilled with an ankle-deep experience when the current of a deep river awaits us! Let's be good stewards of the power with which we're entrusted and move on to a deeper flow.

VISITATIONS FROM GOD

I don't believe it to be coincidental that many of the greatest experiences I've had with God took place in the local church, among the other members of His Body. Of course, I've had experiences with God while alone in prayer, but those are of a different type than the experiences that are available within the local church.

There have been times during a service when God's power has fallen in measures so strong that I was forever changed. If I close my eyes and visualize those meetings, it seems as though I'm right there again. Such God-experiences greatly affect us, becoming landmarks in our lives. I often remember who I was with in those services, and in some cases can recall where people were sitting (or laying, as the case may be). Some of my strongest relationships with others were formed as we were present together during such visitations from God.

During one midweek service at our church, God's power came into the room with such intensity that none of us could move under its weight. I was seated in a chair on our platform; however, my wife was standing on the platform. She was stuck in a trance, unable to move for about an hour. While the purpose of such demonstrations of God's power is a subject worthy of its own book, I'll simply say that we've never been the same after that visitation from God. This visitation didn't occur in a restaurant, shopping center, or theater, but came as believers were gathered together in the local church.

IMPARTATIONS

> For I long to see you, that I may impart to you some spiritual gift to strengthen you.
>
> Romans 1:11

An impartation is a spiritual deposit from God that brings great blessing and benefit. When believers meet together for worship, truth is imparted and revelation is deposited into their hearts. These kinds of impartations can be frequently experienced. However, as this verse reveals, impartations don't occur when people are not *seen*.

One would have to dismiss much of the Bible to avoid recognizing the importance of being physically present where God is moving. Things happen in us and for us when we're present that don't happen when we're absent. The value of these impartations is beyond description and should cause the believer to never want to miss a service.

There have been many times when I've left a service changed; I could sense that something great had been deposited within me. Spiritual impartations can bring direction to a life that's off course, help prevent wrong decisions, and bring understanding where confusion once reigned. Impartations strengthen a life, leading the believer to victory over every kind of bondage. These priceless deposits come when a person is in the habit of being present as believers gather together.

REMOTE MINISTRY

While we're thankful for the role of technology in spreading the gospel, technology has its limitations. Real spirit-to-spirit ministry isn't achieved through a television screen the way it is in person. Some churches in our day are ministering to people exclusively via video screens. While this method of ministry may be somewhat effective, it can never be completely effective.

As popular as they may be, these "satellite" churches have some drawbacks. A video screen (no matter how large) can't compensate for the physical presence of a pastor. Effective ministry in the local church requires that people be seen. Although the people may see the pastor, their pastor can't see them. This means a degree of ministry will be missing; people will have to do without some of the impartations that God has for them. Many aspects of ministry can only be accomplished face-to-face. That's why Paul, even though ministering via a letter, still longed to see the people of the church in Rome.

We can't ignore the supernatural elements of ministry and expect God's plan to be fully accomplished. I'm not opposed to alternative ways of ministering the Gospel. I've ministered extensively on television and have published the gospel through books and recorded media. When it comes to ministry in the local church, however, it's not meant to be a one-sided affair. Many times, the Spirit will tweak a pastor's message as it's being preached in order to help those who are present. This happens in ways so subtle it often goes unnoticed, yet lives can be forever changed. This supernatural element is often missing when the pastor is miles away.

There are times of course when video ministry can be a blessing. Truth broadcast over a screen is always better than doubt and unbelief in person. If there's no Bible-believing pastor and local church in an area, by all means erect the biggest screen possible and pump in the truth. However, it should be the goal to replace the screen with a God-filled pastor as soon as possible. We're not criticizing anyone's efforts in spreading the gospel, but are stressing the point that the flow of God's power is maximized when people gather together. The ministry of a pastor is always most effective in person. Outreaches to the masses are great, but the local church must always remain local. Only then will it be a place of power, visitation, and impartation.

Chapter 14

Visibility and Influence

Our enemy hates everything about the local church, and would love to see every good church close its doors. That's not going to happen, so the devil instead works to keep churches from enjoying a place of prominence. As long as no one can see or find a particular church, Satan is not overly concerned. He works to keep churches from acquiring buildings and lands, especially those that are prominently placed, so he can hide what God wants displayed. How important is it to God that His people and works be visible on the Earth? Consider the following verses:

"You are **the light of the world**. A city **set on a hill** cannot be hidden. Nor do people light a lamp and put it under a basket, but on a stand, and it gives light to all in the house. In the same way, let your light shine before others, so that they may see your good works and give glory to your Father who is in heaven.

Matthew 5:14-16

Great is the Lord and greatly to be praised in the city of our God! His **holy mountain, beautiful in eleva-tion**, is the joy of all the earth, Mount Zion, in the far north, the city of the great King.

Psalm 48:1-2

Listen as Wisdom calls out! Hear as understanding raises her voice! **On the hilltop along the road**, she takes her stand **at the crossroads. By the gates at the entrance to the town, on the road leading in**, she cries aloud.

Proverbs 8:1-3 (NLT)

These verses all place God's works in a place of maximum visibility. There's a place of visibility, prominence, and influence that every pastor should contend for. God desires His churches to enjoy a place of exaltation within their communities. When a building is set on a hilltop, it can be easily seen by all. I understand that the verses above are illustrating spiritual truths, but I believe they also show God's desire for His churches to be well-placed within their communities, both physically and in other ways.

In some countries, it's illegal for a Christian church to even exist. Churches in those places must operate underground. In our country, however, we're privileged to worship openly. Churches in our communities need not hide underground. We're free to acquire buildings, billboards, radio stations, TV stations, and more to help point people toward God; whatever it takes to become visible.

DOTTING THE LANDSCAPE

I like when I come into a town and see churches everywhere. I like it even better when the nicest churches are the ones preaching the Word and flowing with the Spirit. When driving through a town I'm unfamiliar with, churches are my favorite thing to look at.

When we moved to a different part of the country a few years ago, it was impossible not to notice how different the landscape was. We had moved from an area with many hills, lush greenery, and tall trees, to a place that doesn't look like it can grow much of anything (we have great mountain views, however). It took us a little while to get used to the topography.

As I was driving with my wife one day, I commented about a different part of the landscape. "Where are all the churches?" I asked. We had previously lived in a part of the country where there were church buildings everywhere. Many of them were old, and those churches might not have been preaching the Word exactly, but at least they were there. In contrast, the area to which we moved was newer, and churches didn't dot the landscape the way they had in my previous town. I don't like that. I like seeing churches everywhere. The Church is to have a place of visibility.

NEW BUILDINGS

It means something when a church has a place of visibility within the community. A church is wise to seek God as to how it can effectively reach its community. Churches should endeavor to make themselves visible at certain times. One church I attended takes visibility seriously (and quite literally). They place over two million Christmas lights on their property every winter and have a huge fireworks show every summer. They do these things to make themselves visible in their town. Those kinds of things are fine to do as the Lord leads.

Having a church building will also make a church visible. When a church is just beginning, believers may meet in a school or rent space in a retail facility, but as the church grows, a place of their own with greater visibility can enable a greater impact. I have a pastor friend who recently moved his church from one rented facility to another larger rented facility. Because they were moving to a better location, their attendance doubled. They now own the building they were renting.

I understand that the local church is more than just a building, and that the physical presence of a church can be overemphasized. On the other hand, buildings are a necessary part of conducting ministry. Many pastors have smaller congregations and cannot presently occupy a larger facility. That's understandable. The last thing a church needs is to be in a building that overwhelms the congregation financially. Church facilities require a lot of maintenance and can quickly consume resources. Having said that, pastors and congregations must look ahead, exercising their faith for buildings and lands before those facilities are needed.

When a church is just beginning, the members and ministers can begin to exercise faith for the ministry's future buildings and equipment. Learn to believe big, for God's more than able to perform what He's promised. See your church with plenty of His best resources, fully occupied and fully funded. I know of some churches in rented facilities who fill their building every week but don't have any space for expansion and aren't actively seeking a larger space. Small vision, small thinking, and small believing keep them from making movement toward a larger place with greater visibility.

At one point, as Rev. Kenneth E. Hagin sought wisdom in the area of finances, God spoke something interesting to him. The Lord said, "I expect my people to have the nicest place in town to meet in." What a statement! Is it true? Yes. Plenty of scripture agrees with that statement. One need look no further than God's plans for the Old Testament Tabernacle and Temple to see that He desires His people to worship in the nicest possible environment.

Many churches keep their facilities in a state of disrepair. People may think they're deferring repairs because of money problems, but that's not always the issue. In some cases the real problem is a lack of faith and excellence. Sometimes, members expect the pastor to personally perform all the maintenance and upkeep of the church building and grounds. I ministered as a guest in one church where the pastor's wife couldn't eat with us because she had to clean the entire building by herself. That's wrong! There were plenty of people in that church who could have assumed that task but they wouldn't lift a finger to improve the house of God. Shameful! While a church is waiting for the needed funds for repairs or upgrades, they should do all they can to maintain a standard of excellence. Churches must be good stewards of the facility they presently occupy if they are to qualify for a nicer place.

THE CHURCH'S OTHER FRONT DOOR

There are ways a church can increase its visibility without having to raise thousands or millions of dollars. People in most parts of the world search online in order to find a church. It doesn't take a crazy amount of money to have a good-looking website. A website is the virtual front door of a church, yet many choose to ignore this avenue of visibility. Before stepping foot into a local church, most people will browse the church's website. I've viewed the websites of many churches that preach the message of faith. I'm not sure where they use their faith, but they don't use it to make a good first impression on online visitors.

Some leaders don't believe they need an online presence. They say, "I'm going to just let God bring the people in." That's not faith, nor is it reality. Yes, believe God to bring the people, but don't work against Him by hiding your church from the world. God's committed to the visibility of His church and will supply the needed resources to help us represent Him with excellence.

A PLACE OF INFLUENCE

One reason society ignores the Church is that we've been willing to forfeit our place of influence. The Church is a force to be reckoned with in our world, and there are times when we must stand up and make our presence known.

In the area in which I formerly pastored, the Catholic Church was king. Anyone who ran for political office (and was wise) would find a priest and take him along on the campaign trail. In my town, if the Catholic Church didn't like you, you weren't going very far. Their place of influence was tremendous, and it helped give the other churches in our area a greater place of influence and respect. Ministers shouldn't be begging town and city governments for attention; those governments should be calling the pastors, asking for help and wisdom. The churches in my town regularly interacted with our town government to affect positive change.

I understand that people in certain parts of the country are less willing to recognize the value of the local church in society, but their incorrect perceptions can change. It would help if all in the Church would work to bring dignity and respect to the house of God. Let's believe together for the local church to be the place of visibility and influence that God desires.

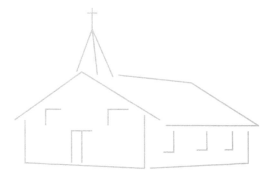

CHAPTER 15

Provision and Connection

The local church is the base from which the majority of all ministry activities proceed. The Gospel to the world is largely funded through the local church. Local churches are poised to reach out in service to their local communities. And when a church member finds themselves in a place of difficulty, they have a family to turn to: their local church. The church is a hub for all the things of God and is a place of provision, connection, and service.

THE STOREHOUSE

> Bring the full tithe into the storehouse, that there may be food in my house. And thereby put me to the test, says the Lord of hosts, if I will not open the windows of heaven for you and pour down for you a blessing until there is no more need.
>
> Malachi 3:10

What is *the storehouse* spoken of in this verse? It can only be the local church. The local church is a place of provision; a place through which God's resources can flow. Most local churches today, however, have very little "food in the house." They have difficulty funding their own existence, much less funding other projects and outreaches. Why does lack exist in the house of God? One reason is the Body of Christ's failure to emphasize tithes and offerings.

I would have difficulty attending or recommending a church where there was little or no preaching about money. There are over two thousand references to money (and its proper use) in Scripture. These are in the Bible so believers might know them and put them into practice in their lives. Many churches in our day have deemphasized the Bible's teaching about money and giving so as to not offend any among them. Such decisions are often made with people's comfort in mind, but catering to temporal comfort can rob people of long-term blessing. Leaders must seek God and His Word, allowing Him to dictate the content of their ministry. He will, at least occasionally, lead ministers to preach the Word regarding money.

The *full tithe* is to be brought into the storehouse, making the church a place of abundant provision. If everyone in a church would bring their tithe, every need would be met and that church would have reserves in place for the Lord's discretionary use. It's not God's plan for the church to lack in any area.

For the first several years of my Christian life, I was around believers who only quoted one verse about money, and they quoted it incorrectly. *Money is the root of all evil*, is what I often heard. Although that's not what this verse actually says (see 1 Timothy 6:10), that was the summary statement of the financial beliefs of my first church. They believed that if it cost money, it had to be bad. That church was always broke (and all the people were broke) because they were convinced that money was a curse.

I'll never forget my shock and amazement when I started to be among people of the Word and faith. During one large meeting, a special offering was received for the host ministry, with minister after minister presenting checks from their churches for many thousands of dollars. One particular minister was testifying about how the truths he received from this ministry had blessed his life. As he presented a check for one hundred thousand dollars he said, "The Word of God has so blessed us that our church facility is paid for, all our equipment is paid for, and we have a million dollars in the bank just waiting for God to tell us what to do with it."

Some would find fault with such a scene, but not me. Large sums of money flowing in and out of the local church is one of the most godly things I've ever witnessed. When a church can single-handedly plant another church, or underwrite a missions project, it's godly. Great provision should flow through the local church, and it's God's plan that it come through the people as they're obedient to give.

The tithe (one-tenth of your income) belongs to God. It's the starting point for a lifestyle of giving and receiving. If a believer misses a service, the amount of their tithe should not decrease; you don't keep it just because you're not present to give it. It still belongs to God. It's not right for a Christian to withhold their tithe. When a person, through unbelief or stinginess, withholds what they should give, there's a sense in which they are withholding the Gospel message from someone who has yet to hear.

BRING THE TITHE TO THE CHURCH

Some preach that the tithe ought not be limited to the local church, but can be given anywhere the believer desires (or not given at all if the believer is in a time of need). While I agree that our giving is to be God-directed, God *has* directed us in His Word to bring all the tithe *into the storehouse*. One cannot point to any institution other than the local church as the storehouse: the distribution center for God's funds. Notice also, the tithe is to be *brought*, not sent somewhere else. It goes where you go: to the local church.

While it's true that the Bible speaks of many forms of giving, the tithe to the local church comes first. Other kinds of giving happen after the tithe. The tithe belongs *to* God, but belongs *at* the local church. It's important that the local church be taken care of before anything else. It's also right that the believer respond to the leading of the Spirit to give in other ways, funding other ministries that God is promoting, as well as giving to other people.

It's worth noting that the Apostle Paul, when receiving an offering for the believers at Jerusalem, didn't do so secretly or through a ministry of his own, but received it publicly through the local churches. God will bring a supply to Christians so they're able to give to the various projects He is funding. Much of this giving can be efficiently processed through the ministries of the local church.

When the church has a ministry project that needs to be funded, get excited and get involved. If it means waiting on a desire of your own a little while longer, so be it. After your tithe, do all you can to help eliminate every need in the local church.

During the years I pastored, I did my best to teach the people their responsibilities in the area of giving (and the blessings that would result). As they responded to God's Word, our church was able to support missionaries, help plant other churches, and engage in regular partnership with traveling ministries. It's the believer's privilege to do their part to make the local church a place of provision.

A PLACE OF CONNECTION

The local church is where believers connect with others who share their faith. There's no better network than the community of the local church. It's sad that many who profess Christ still look for companionship in places like bars or nightclubs. The church is the place in which to develop godly relationships. We don't attend church just to find a potential spouse, of course, but the right person for our lives will find us as we remain connected in the church in which God has placed us.

I've watched Christian ladies leave our church because they felt there were not enough eligible men attending. That's not sound thinking, nor is it a valid reason to join or leave a church. With some of those ladies, a single man their age began attending soon after they left. It's possible he might have been the one that one of them was looking for. Notice that God didn't send him where she was. He sent him where she should have been. We must be satisfied where God has placed us, understanding that He can bring the right person to us at the right time.

When I was first saved, I only knew a few Christians. I longed for Christian fellowship, but because I wasn't connected to a local church, my desire for fellowship remained unfulfilled. As soon as I connected to my local church, I discovered that I now had a family (as well as a pastor). I didn't stay at this church because the doctrine was perfect (I didn't even know what doctrine was). I stayed because the people loved and cared for me. I was connected to a family of believers and learned just how powerful that connection could be.

It's so important to be properly connected. There are several ways in which the local church acts as a place of connection for the believer. While we've already spoken about the tithe, many don't realize that, besides supplying material provision, tithing creates a spiritual connection with one's church. The spiritual act of tithing connects a believer to his or her pastor in a greater way, allowing the believer to receive more from the pastor's ministry. It's not that we're buying the pastor's favor (or buying anything), rather we're connecting to the spiritual supply that God has for us.

God is a God of connections. He loves to orchestrate things for our good, connecting us with people that will bless our lives and placing us in situations that help us fulfill His plan. These things don't happen as they should when we're out of our assigned place in His Body. When we were spiritually lost, God found us and brought us to Himself. Once we're saved, however, He expects us to be in the place He's planted us: the local church of His choosing. That's where His blessing will be. We're always in the right place when we're in our local church.

Some of the most successful, committed, and happy Christians I've known are those whose lives revolved around their local church. I'm not saying these people neglect their home life, families, or other duties, but their connection with their church is so strong that even their social life revolves around the church. They're always thinking about how they can enhance the house of God and bless their pastor and fellow church members. For the fulfilled Christian, there's no place like the local church.

Far too many believers are only partially connected at church. They're like a lamp that has become unplugged, with the cord dangling in the socket by just one prong. Every now and then they receive a flicker of light, but not the steady flow of blessing that God has for them. Be completely plugged in, unwilling to be removed from your place of connection: your local church.

SERVICE

> For God is not unjust so as to overlook your work and the love that you have shown for his name in **serving the saints**, as you still do.
>
> Hebrews 6:10

The activities of the local church provide opportunities for the Christian to serve others. There are some churches that excel in serving, but don't preach or teach anything that spiritually feeds people. Their service is in the flesh and could just as easily be accomplished by a civic organization. On the other hand, some churches preach a great message, but do nothing else. A church must be balanced, excelling in all areas of ministry (see 2 Corinthians 8:7). The inward-focused church positions itself for decline rather than increase.

There are many who desire to serve God, but their ministry involvement only takes place outside the local church. That's unwise. It's not acceptable to serve elsewhere while neglecting your responsibilities at your own church. Some might say, "I don't have any responsibilities at my church." Yes, you do. You may have not yet discovered them, but God exempts no one from involvement in the local church. Simply attending is not enough. Involvement and commitment is where it's at.

STAY WITH YOUR PASTOR

If a person in a local church feels led to volunteer with another local ministry, he or she should submit that decision to their pastor (or the pastor's representative) to make sure the pastor also feels right about it. I lived in an area for many years that had several non-church ministries headquartered close by. Most of them desired volunteer help from the neighboring local churches. I knew some of them to be safe places for my members to go, but there were others that I preferred them to stay away from.

Our town had a Christian television station that was a real blessing to the community. That station required a great deal of volunteer help to operate, and I didn't mind our church members helping as long as their church involvement didn't suffer. I told our people they would be welcome to get involved there. I later realized I should have been more specific.

One gentleman at our church chose to volunteer at the TV station on Wednesday nights, during our midweek service. He had been a moderately committed member of our church, but I knew he wasn't a fan of the deeper flow that we had on Wednesdays. This man didn't realize that by volunteering during our service, he was occupying a place of ministry out of the will of God. To regularly miss services at your own church in order to serve elsewhere is wrong, unless the pastor gives his blessing to it.

I didn't try to stop this man when I found out why he was no longer attending church on Wednesdays. He had been under my ministry for years and knew better, but was free to make his own decisions. He could sense my disapproval when he told me what he was doing, but didn't care. People often neglect their own church to serve other places. They fail to count the cost of devaluing their local church, not realizing that this type of disregard carries negative consequences. In this gentleman's case, he died suddenly at a young age. One can't help but wonder if his story would have had a happier ending had he remained more closely connected at church. We must all learn to bring appropriate honor to our God-assigned place.

I know of a situation where a prominent minister launched a new church in a certain area. There was a neighboring church that had, on several occasions, hosted this minister as a guest. When the new church opened, the older church lost many of the people who served in their Ministry of Helps. They all went to serve the well-known minister with whom they were enthralled and forsook their own church (and the pastor that had given so much of his time to their care). Such examples reveal that many people have no revelation at all of the importance of the local church—*their* local church.

When a popular minister comes to town, don't leave your

church to go see him or her. I don't care if Jesus Himself is ministering at a nearby church on a Sunday morning. Go see Him when your church is not meeting (and only go if it's someone your pastor would be okay with, like Jesus). Pay attention to which ministers and ministries your pastor speaks of, and feed on their material as a supplement to—not a replacement for—your pastor's teaching. A big issue within the local church is that people feed on everything except their pastor's teaching.

My church knew exactly which ministries I recommended because I often spoke of how those ministries had impacted my life. I didn't speak against other ministries, but the fact that I never referred to them as an influence in my life should have sent the message. It's not that other ministries are bad or in error, but not all are going the same direction. Exposing oneself to a wide variety of visions or directions can bring confusion to a person's spirit and weaken their connection to their local church.

This is a bigger issue than many realize. Some might think the pastor who addresses these things has a controlling spirit or is insecure. No, it's not an insecurity issue, it's a maturity issue. These ethical and honor issues must be taught in the local church. The pastor who is mature in God will teach these things in order to protect those under his care. People often put more stock in what the television minister preaches than what their pastor preaches. I know people do this innocently, but it's still wrong. There are indeed excellent ministries on television, but none are to have as strong a voice in your life as your pastor. It's the church member's responsibility to keep these areas in order. It's fine to feed on good, faith-building materials, but we must exercise caution regarding what we watch or read.

There were times when members of my congregation would pass around books written by prominent ministers. Some of these books were full of unbelief and false teaching, yet were widely embraced because the minister was popular. It's difficult to lead a church into spiritual progress when the people are feeding on everything except the pastor's teaching. It's challenging to maintain spiritual effectiveness when people in the church are feeding on tainted spiritual food.

The reason I knew what was in these books was that I would occasionally be handed a copy. A church member would say, "Pastor, here's a book for you to read. It's great." That member may have been well meaning but their actions were out of place. The church member should view the pastor as their teacher and themselves as the student, not the other way around. Instead of assigning your pastor books to read, it would be better to say, "Pastor, I'm interested in such-and-such. Do you know of any books I could read on that subject?" Feed on what your pastor feeds on, and you'll remain safe and well-connected.

This doesn't mean the pastor is unapproachable or infallible, or that he or she could never learn anything from a church member. There are things I've learned from church members, but it was always as the person was serving in his or her place; never when they were trying to usurp my place.

I recall a now-humorous incident where a church member asked to meet with me after a service. He began the conversation by saying, "Pastor, turn in your Bible to such-and-such scripture," and proceeded to correct me. This is backward (that person later apologized). It's not the church member's place to bring correction to their pastor or to teach him or her or influence their beliefs. The pastor should have others in their life that they look to: seasoned ministers through whom God is able to bring instruction and correction as needed. God will use those individuals long before He uses the church member who thinks he or she is more enlightened than their pastor.

Being properly connected is everything for the believer. Your health, provision, and safety depend on you being in your place in the Body of Christ. Stay connected—involved and engaged—to your local church and you'll have access to all of God's best, all the time.

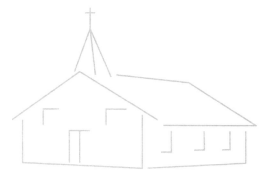

CHAPTER 16

Salvation, Prayer, and Healing

There are few places on Earth where a person can have their life instantly and permanently changed. The local church is one of those places. It's a place where the needs of the believer can be met, but it's also a place where the lost can find salvation. Where else can a person be guaranteed to find eternal life? The Church must be ever ready to help the hungry soul receive God's living water so that he or she may thirst no more.

Of course, people can receive Christ anywhere. I was saved in a car at the beach. Every Christian is encouraged to be active in leading people to Christ, sharing with them, praying with them, and following up with them. The soul-winning Christian must also be diligent to bring these new converts to church. The church for the new believer is what the hospital nursery is to a newborn baby. A baby will never thrive if left alone, nor will the new Christian survive or thrive without the local church.

> Like newborn infants, long for the pure spiritual milk, that by it you may grow up into salvation.
>
> 1 Peter 2:2

Where does the baby Christian find the nourishment that he or she needs? It can only come from the local church. That's where he or she will be joined to their pastor, receive from the Word, and experience the anointing. It's where they will connect with other believers and enjoy the protection only God can bring. It's not fair for a person to be born again and not be given the opportunity to grow and develop. The opportunity for spiritual development is primarily found in the local church.

I'm reminded of a Sunday morning when a member of our congregation came to church bubbling with excitement. He shared that during the weekend, he was involved in leading dozens of people to the Lord. When he said that, I looked around the building and asked, "Where are they?" Not one of these new converts came to church (I'm pretty sure he never invited any of them). This man didn't understand why I didn't share his excitement.

I was excited that he had that opportunity, but it's debatable whether getting people to pray a prayer, then leaving them to fend for themselves spiritually really accomplishes anything. Spiritual infants can't grow and mature until they're fed in the local church; left alone, they'll receive little or no nourishment. If we treated a human baby that way, he or she would quickly die. What do we expect will happen with these spiritual newborns?

This man soon left our church to find one that was more *on fire*, where his gifts would be celebrated. He probably thought we had no passion for souls, but the opposite is true. We're passionate about seeing spiritual babies born, then watching them thrive. Go out and get all the people saved you can. Just complete the transaction by bringing them to church and helping them become established in the things of God.

A PLACE OF PRAYER

> And he was teaching them and saying to them, "Is it not written, 'My house shall be called **a house of prayer** for all the nations'? But you have made it a

den of robbers."

Mark 11:17

Many think of the church as a house of prayer only in terms of people coming to receive prayer. Many churches have a prayer ministry where members of the body pray for the needs of others. While there's value to this type of ministry, I don't believe that's the full emphasis of this verse. There are ways to pray that are more effective than simply fielding the prayer requests of others.

In what way, then, is the local church a house of prayer? It's not just a place where we pray for others, but a place of corporate prayer. It's important that believers learn to pray together, as a body. This is an unfamiliar concept to many. While the bulk of the believer's praying may be done alone, the church has a responsibility to take its place in prayer together. Notice this example of the Early Church praying during a time of intense persecution:

> And when they heard it, **they lifted their voices together to God** and said, "Sovereign Lord, who made the heaven and the earth and the sea and everything in them. . . . look upon their threats and grant to your servants to continue to speak your word with all boldness, while you stretch out your hand to heal, and signs and wonders are performed through

the name of your holy servant Jesus."

Acts 4:24, 29-30

This picture of the New Testament Church at prayer shows the believers drawing upon the help of the Spirit to pray. They prayed out loud, all at once, each one tapping into the help of the Holy Spirit within them. One way the church can pray together is when all lift their voice and pray in other tongues. That may be what the believers did here, and it's an effective way to pray. The Bible doesn't record every word that was spoken, but rather records the essence of what was prayed by all. Notice how their time of prayer concluded:

> And when they had prayed, the place in which they were gathered together was shaken, and they were all filled with the Holy Spirit and continued to speak the word of God with boldness.

Acts 4:31

One thing is certain, good things happen when believers pray. Here in Acts, the lives of those present were positively affected, the needed answer was received, and so much power was made available that the building shook. When believers make spiritual movement and God's glory permeates the atmosphere, the results can often be felt in the natural realm. We need more results in the natural realm; we need more building-shaking prayer! Here's another example of the Early Church united in prayer:

> So Peter was kept in prison, but earnest prayer for him was made to God by the church.
>
> Acts 12:5

When one of the key leaders of the Church was in jeopardy, the Church prayed. As a result, an angel came and sprung Peter out of prison. When Peter then went to the gathering place of the believers, they were still there, taking their place together in prayer.

> When he realized this, he went to the house of Mary, the mother of John whose other name was Mark, where many were gathered together and were praying.
>
> Acts 12:12

The church coming together in prayer is a great necessity. Many churches fall short in this area. We need the power of God in manifestation, yet that doesn't happen without a spiritual supply being created through prayer. Of course, just one person taking their place in prayer is powerful, but that power can be multiplied as believers come together. We must not neglect the power-producing effect of prayer.

> Confess to one another therefore your faults (your slips, your false steps, your offenses, your sins) and pray [also] for one another, that you may be healed and restored [to a spiritual tone of mind and heart]. The earnest (heartfelt, continued) prayer of a righteous man **makes tremendous power available** [dynamic in its working].
>
> James 5:16 (AMP)

God's power can be made available in our midst where it will work dynamically. Power from Heaven is always potentially available, but the right kind of prayer brings that power into manifestation, placing it within easy reach of those who need it. I'm convinced that the presence of God's manifested power is the missing element in many churches today. It's the reason why results are scarce in some places.

Rev. Kenneth E. Hagin would tell how his church would meet for services on Sunday mornings, as well as Sunday evenings. In those days, only his church members would attend the morning service while the evening service would be filled with people who were seekers, or unsaved. The church would flow with God's Spirit (sometimes in prayer) on Sunday mornings until the atmosphere was charged with God's power. Then, on Sunday night, that power manifested to minister to those present. Convicting power to save manifested, and the lost would respond. There was also great power to heal.

When believers unite in prayer and faith, sickness doesn't stand a chance. The local church has been ordained as a place of healing, deliverance, and freedom. A person who is bound can get answers and help at church that they won't find anywhere else. The anointing of the pastor's office, combined with the anointing upon the congregation, will bring God's mighty power on the scene. Go to church to get free. Go to church for deliverance and healing. Then stay in the local church to keep what you've found and help others receive the same.

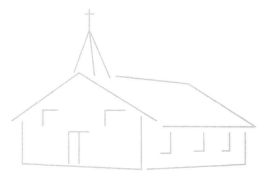

CHAPTER 17

Your Pastor

Perhaps the most important reason to never let anything keep you from your local church is that your pastor is there. It's essential to be present with your pastor as he or she ministers, for their anointing doesn't operate via audio or video the same way it operates in person. In-person ministry features dimensions of impartation and blessing that distanced ministry does not. The pastor's anointing is an amazing thing—a gift from God—and will lead those who remain under it to maturity. The great benefits found in the local church exist largely because the pastor is there.

The pastor is the main one through whom the Spirit brings

revelation, correction, and direction. The pastor's ministry provides opportunities for development, growth, and feeding. His care offers safety and protection. The pastor is to be respected and revered, for what's in him or her is precious and irreplaceable. He or she is not God, but serves as God's representative to the believers in his or her care. Thank God for the pastor.

YOU NEED A PASTOR

> When He saw the throngs, He was moved with pity and sympathy for them, because they were bewildered (harassed and distressed and dejected and helpless), like sheep without a shepherd.
>
> Matthew 9:36 (AMP)

The Greek word translated as *shepherd* is the same word translated as *pastor*. We could read the last part of this verse this way: *they were like people without a pastor*. These words of Jesus show what will become of those who disconnect from their local church and pastor. They will be *harassed, distressed, dejected, and helpless*. Let's study these words individually to discover the full importance of the pastor's place.

When someone is *harassed*, they endure unrelenting pestering and attack. We've all heard of harassment in the workplace where one worker makes unwanted comments or advances toward another. The believer who remains outside his or her local church and pastor will likewise be harassed by the enemy. The enemy will have a level of access into his or her life that he doesn't have in the life of one who is committed and connected in their local church. God has made provision for the believer to be free from harassment by placing a pastor in his or her life.

People are *distressed* when things aren't working right or going well. Make no mistake: things won't go well for the Christian who is disconnected from their local church. On the other hand, the life that rightly connects to the local church and pastor is not a distressed life, but one that can enjoy the full measure of the peace of God. Notice that the word *distressed* includes the word *stress*. Our lives are not meatn to bear stress and carry cares. Have you ever seen distressed furniture? It looks like somebody beat on it and marked it up. Too many Christians are beat up and marked with defeat. Get in church, in an atmosphere of God's peace, where the enemy can't beat you up or take advantage of you.

To understand what it means to be *dejected*, watch as a television camera pans the bench of a sports team that knows they're about to lose the biggest game of the season. People are down and dejected when they suffer loss. Christians who live apart from the local church will know well what it means to suffer loss in life; but not those with a pastor. The pastor could be considered a loss mitigation officer in the believer's life. He or she helps the believer possess and retain all that's theirs, and will show him or her how to live victoriously.

The word *helpless* describes many in the Body of Christ. The helpless individual is a frustrated soul. No matter what they do, they can't seem to make progress. We must understand that we all need help; particularly the help that our pastor brings to our lives. We also need the help and blessing that comes from interacting with others in the Body of Christ. If we'll access the help that's ours, we won't be helpless.

The person without a pastor—harassed, distressed, dejected, and helpless—will not enjoy a victorious life. While difficult situations and circumstances may occasionally present themselves, the Christian without a pastor is ill-equipped for victory. Yes, he or she may have the Word, the Spirit, and faith, but that's not enough! Without a pastor, the believer will be unable to successfully navigate life's challenges. Believers should not blame the devil for failures that ensue when a person removes him or herself from their local church and pastor. The blame lies with the believer alone.

COMPLETE

> And you are complete in Him, who is the head of all
> principality and power.
>
> Colossians 2:10 (NKJV)

To be complete *in Him* means that we're complete *in Christ*. In other words, we're complete *in our place in Christ's Body*: rightly connected with others, including our pastor and fellow church members. If we're out of place, we're incomplete or deficient. The Christian without a pastor is an incomplete Christian who cannot complete his or her race in life. There's no reason for the believer to be helpless or incomplete when God has provided a measure of help that completes them.

I'm not suggesting that believers are to overly depend on their pastor, nor am I diminishing the ability of believers to receive help from God on their own. I'm simply illustrating how God intends for the pastor's anointing to benefit the believer's life, and how the absence of that anointing will create a void in the believer's life.

The failure rate among Christians in marriage, business, and other endeavors is sky high and there's no good reason for it. Success is not that difficult, but it requires the one thing that many seem incapable of: remaining connected to one's local church and pastor. I refuse to be removed from my pastor. I won't take a job that pulls me away from my pastor (unless my pastor and I agree that God's in it). I won't retire and move to a tropical island where I'm separated from my pastor. The absence of a pastor guarantees failure in the Christian's life. Let's do the math and be successful: God plus the pastor plus me equals success.

MORE PASTORS NEEDED

> When he saw the crowds, he had compassion for them, because they were harassed and helpless, like sheep without a shepherd. Then he said to his disciples, "The harvest is plentiful, but **the laborers are few**; therefore pray earnestly to the Lord of the harvest to **send out laborers** into his harvest."
>
> Matthew 9:37-38

Compassion for people led Jesus to give a prayer assignment to His followers. Notice that He didn't tell them to pray that people would be strengthened to make it through. He didn't tell them to ask God to establish a network of counseling centers or telephone prayer lines. No, Jesus had them pray that laborers (workers or ministers) would be sent into harvest fields where the people are. Every time a pastor goes to a city to establish a local church, this prayer is being answered.

We must continue to pray this prayer today, for people remain harassed and helpless, living far below the victory that's theirs. Most cities and towns have several churches, but many do not have even one church that really understands how to minister the Word and flow with the Spirit. There are places throughout town where one can go for coffee or shopping or liquor, but are there places where one can find salvation, healing, or deliverance? A great need in our day is more strong churches, led by pastors who will faithfully lead their people to success.

LEARNING TO LOVE YOUR PASTOR

> Saul also went to his home at Gibeah, and with him went men of valor whose hearts God had touched.
>
> 1 Samuel 10:26

This verse moves me every time I read it. There's something precious about the way God joins people to those He's appointed for leadership. Notice that the relationship between King Saul and his helpers wasn't just a relationship between men; it was God-initiated.

God can't touch everyone's heart as He did with these men of valor, because not every heart is sensitive to God's touch. The person of valor, honor, and character, however, can sense God's dealings, see beyond the surface, and understand the depths of a relationship. We need people today in the local church who are sensitive to God's touch where their pastor is concerned.

As I was growing up, there were school teachers I liked and those I didn't like. All of my teachers had a similar measure of authority, but a few of them made such an investment into my life that I felt a strong connection with them. To put it another way, some of my teachers had my heart while others did not.

Mrs. Goodheart was my least favorite teacher in high school. I'll never know what possessed me to take her Advanced Humanities class. I gave her the compulsory level of respect she was due, but really didn't like her. I didn't like Mrs. Goodheart because she challenged us and didn't allow us to just slide by. She made us earn our grade (which I did not). Although I didn't like her then, I now think of her often, wishing I had paid better attention in her class (especially when she was correcting my writing assignments).

Many view their pastor the way I viewed Mrs. Goodheart. They see their pastor as someone who occupies a place of authority or leadership, but they don't give him or her their heart. Mrs. Goodheart never had my heart, which is why I barely got anything out of her class except a poor grade. Likewise, the person who withholds their heart from their pastor will only receive from his ministry in a limited measure.

When God places a person in a local church, He's joining him or her to a pastor. God will touch the heart of that church member toward his or her pastor, helping them grasp the full importance of the pastor's place. We must recognize the anointing on the pastor's office, understanding that the pastor is more to us than just a fellow man or woman. God wants us so impressed with the greatness of the pastor's place that we value, respect, and receive from it.

The church member should learn to love their pastor, giving him or her a place of high esteem in their heart. Of course, I'm not speaking of a romantic or natural love. Members must be careful not to misinterpret God's touch as a physical or emotional love. The love of which I'm speaking is a precious spiritual intertwining that has little to do with natural qualities like the pastor's personality. One need not even like their pastor's personality to develop a love for their anointing and place of ministry.

Some might consider this teaching to be extreme, but it's not. It's just not taught very often, which is why it's understood by few people. The Body of Christ finds itself lacking in this area. Many Christians don't know their pastor well (in a spiritual sense) and therefore don't bring the level of care that they should to his or her life and ministry. Church members should allow God to knit their hearts to their pastor, endeavoring to see him as the blessing he is. The person who does this will be amazed at how things change for them.

Of the many church members I was privileged to pastor, only a few gave me their hearts. Many liked me, but few loved me. I could have blessed their lives in greater ways had they given me a prominent place in their hearts. The ones under my watch who let the Lord touch their hearts enjoyed success and saw increase in their lives. The ones who never gave me their hearts never seemed to make much spiritual progress.

Allow God to touch your heart where your pastor is concerned. Develop a love, care, and concern for their life and ministry. Make your pastor's vision and mission yours. Find ways to minister back to your pastor, considering all the ways he or she ministers to you. Develop a mindset that if it's important to your pastor, it's important to you. As you do these things, you'll receive from the pastor's ministry in greater ways.

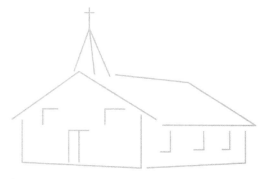

CHAPTER 18

Authority and Rebellion

> Shepherd the flock of God that is among you, **exercising oversight**, not under compulsion, but willingly, as God would have you; not for shameful gain, but eagerly; not domineering over those in your charge, but being examples to the flock.
>
> 1 Peter 5:2-3

People can be in a good church with a good pastor, yet still not receive all the benefits of their pastor's ministry. While we've already discussed some of the reasons this might be, there's another reason worth discussing: the pastor's place of authority. People must have a proper understanding of the pastor's place in order to receive from his or her anointing. Many who haven't been taught in this area simply see the pastor as a man or a friend. Such people will only benefit from the pastor's humanity rather than receiving the full benefit from their ministry. The pastor is specially anointed to minister, and that anointing must be recognized and received by the believer.

The pastor's primary job is to speak into the life of the believer, delivering to him or her the things of God. The pastor is not to try to force the believer's obedience, nor is he to try to run the believer's life or make decisions for the believer. As powerful as the pastor's place is, it's a place of limited authority. While it's the pastor's responsibility to boldly minister, it's the believer's responsibility to receive from and submit to the pastor, recognizing and respecting their place of authority. The passage below speaks to this truth.

> We ask you, brothers, to respect those who labor among you and are over you in the Lord and admonish you, and to esteem them very highly in love because of their work. Be at peace among yourselves.
>
> 1 Thessalonians 5:12-13

REBELLION

Some believers live in opposition to the instruction they're receiving, unaware that the result will be opposition in their own lives. They may think of their disobedience as a justified exception, or an acceptable alternative to the pastor's preaching, but the Bible calls such action *rebellion* (see 1 Samuel 15). Furthermore, the Bible likens rebellion to witchcraft, a practice of those who worship Satan. We certainly wouldn't want to be caught practicing witchcraft. Most Christians would steer clear of a service where Satan is worshipped. Are we just as vigilant to avoid rebellion?

If the pastor doesn't control the believer's life, how is it possible to rebel against him? When a person discounts the pastor's place (who he is) or the pastor's voice (what he says), they're in rebellion. When we rebel against God's representatives (like our pastor), we rebel against Him.

THE REBELLION NON-INVITE

> Adonijah sacrificed sheep, oxen, and fattened cattle by the Serpent's Stone, which is beside En-rogel, and he invited all his brothers, the king's sons, and all the royal officials of Judah, but **he did not invite Nathan the prophet** or Benaiah or the mighty men or Solomon his brother.
>
> 1 Kings 1:9-10

When we fail to invite the man of God into our plans, it can indicate rebellion. Adonijah, recognizing that his father David was ailing, appointed himself to succeed him on the throne. He held a coronation ceremony, but didn't invite the people who would have opposed him or the anointing that would have exposed him. Solomon was the rightful heir to the throne, not Adonijah. Adonijah was just playing king.

Many behave similarly when, like Adonijah, they manufacture a promotion or exaltation in their mind. They call it a "word from God" and try to make it come to pass. All along, they're perpetuating their own plans rather than God's. They don't share their plans with their pastor because they think, *Surely, the pastor is not spiritual enough to pick up on this great and unique calling I've received. After all, he's often failed to recognize my gifts in the past. Why would he recognize this?* Such thinking is dangerous and, of course, unscriptural. This type of situation often occurs today, just like it did in the day of Adonijah.

Understand this: the person who is unwilling to invite the counsel of his or her elders—especially their pastor—when making major life-decisions is flirting with rebellion. That means he or she is on Satan's side, not God's side. The person over on the devil's territory is subject to the devil and can be attacked by him. That's not the place of safety we've talked about. If a person can't submit their plans (especially plans for marriage or ministry) to their pastor, they're almost certainly out of the will of God and headed for trouble.

EXCLUDING THE PASTOR FROM YOUR PLANS

A few of the people in the church I pastored had their own ministries that met on weeknights. These individuals sometimes invited others from our church to attend their meetings (I wondered why attendance was low in our midweek service). In most cases, these church members never told me what they were doing; I usually found out from someone else. These dear people may not have meant to be rebellious, but there's a sense in which they were. I'm sure in their mind they thought nothing of it. That's the problem: they didn't think. They never thought about how their meeting could pull people away from the local church, and because they refused to seek the counsel of their pastor, they remained ignorant on the matter.

What does it matter if other people in the church are having their own services? They're ministering to others and teaching them the Word. Isn't that a good thing? Generally, yes, but these types of member-led ministries should be submitted to the authority of the pastor. It's not right if they're not. Getting together with others for fellowship and discussing the things of God is one thing, but organizing ministry sessions among the members of a local church without involving the leadership of that church is wrong. People don't see it that way, but the person who claims they're "obeying God" while bypassing their pastor is just plain wrong. To put it more plainly, they're in rebellion.

I've known of situations where church members got married without the counsel of their pastor. Friends, if you can't invite the pastor's counsel into a relationship, it's not a relationship you want. When a church member says, "Sorry I wasn't here on Sunday, I got married over the weekend," a pastor doesn't need to pray about whether it's a right or wrong relationship; it's wrong. That person let their flesh do the talking and didn't want the pastor to quench their excitement by interjecting sound wisdom into their impulsive plans. I've seen such marriages end after just a few weeks.

When a person pulls away from a Spirit-filled, Spirit-led pastor, they're likely in error. When your pastor becomes your enemy and you tell your family, "Don't say anything about this to Pastor. In fact, it's best if we just stay away from the church for a while," you know you're in rebellion. There's no such thing as *God spoke to me to do this, but I'm not supposed to talk to my pastor about it.* If it was God who told you, your pastor will be able to confirm it. The pastor's recognition and confirmation of God's plan is something the believer should welcome, not reject.

People who operate deceptively will try to make up for their rebellion in other ways. Some will give extra offerings to try to smooth things over with God. That's what Adonijah did. He brought sacrifice after sacrifice with him to the ceremony to convince himself and everyone else that God was in it. People do similar things today.

Here's what the Bible says about trying to compensate for rebellion:

> And Samuel said, "Has the Lord as great delight in burnt offerings and sacrifices, as in obeying the voice of the Lord? Behold, **to obey is better than sacrifice, and to listen than the fat of rams.** For rebellion is as the sin of divination, and presumption is as iniquity and idolatry. Because you have rejected the word of the Lord, he has also rejected you from being king."
>
> 1 Samuel 15:22-23

INNER REBELLION

Besides manifesting outwardly through a person's actions, rebellion can also exist inwardly in a person's heart. Half of a congregation can be in rebellion together against the pastor while sitting quietly in their seats. As I've ministered to people, I could discern that although they were nodding their heads in agreement, their hearts were spitting out everything I said. A rebellious heart is a dangerous thing.

I once saw a person walking around with something that

looked like an old tape recorder strapped across their shoulder. I found out that it was a monitor that was recording the activity of the person's heart for later analysis. The indwelling Holy Spirit is our spiritual heart monitor. He'll give us constant feedback regarding the condition of our inner man, and will often lead us to make corrections and adjustments. Heed and respond to His warnings, for He's always looking to keep us in a place of safety and receptivity to God.

MINISTRY OR STUPIDITY?

I know of one case where a so-called "prophetess" spent several weeks ministering at a church. During every service, she used her "prophetic gifting" to publicly expose rebellion that she perceived in certain church memebers. She said she was trying to leave the pastor with a clean church. She actually left him with no church (I guess she didn't know the difference between cleaning and clearing, because she cleared that church right out). We must use wisdom and discretion in these areas. What she did wasn't ministry—it was stupidity, and it was ungodly.

The Spirit of God will rarely (if ever) lead a minister to have services where the primary purpose is to expose the rebellion of others. All of us have flesh to deal with and must learn to keep our attitude in check. If God was looking to publicly expose these things, I'm sure I'd be the first one exposed! When a pastor perceives rebellion in a person, it doesn't mean that pastor should confront the person or try to force their repentance. Remember, faith and love don't force. Pastors must be led by the Holy Spirit in their dealings with church members, and must share the Lord's patience rather than being overzealous with correction.

There are times, however, when a pastor may have to confront rebellion in the lives of some of the people in his church. The Lord has prompted me at times to deal with certain ones in my church (these were people who were in open disobedience to the Word and had already been spoken to). He dealt with me in one instance to return a couple's tithe. This was a sizeable gift, and I could have used the money in the church, but if God won't receive someone's offering, I have no right to keep it. I met with them privately, and with a spirit of love shared what God had told me. When I returned this couple's check, they were stunned and looked at me like I had hit them over the head with a baseball bat. Instead of responding with a belligerent spirit of rebellion, this couple softened their hearts in repentance. They made the needed changes in their life and were restored to fellowship. In this couple's case, although their actions were misaligned with God's Word, their hearts were tender toward Him. God can help people like that.

Let's allow love, honesty, and submission to guide our relationship with God, our church, and our pastor. Let's avoid rebellion and submit to the authority of those God has placed over us.

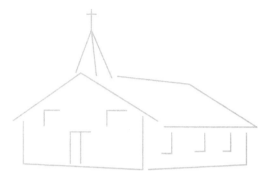

Chapter 19

Embracing Offense

The local church is a place of supreme importance. Every Christian must guard and protect their relationship with their church and pastor. Although a believer may recognize the importance of their place of feeding, the devil will still try to contest it. Satan wants every Christian removed from his or her local church. Although his power to accomplish that removal is limited, he can present thoughts and suggestions to the believer's mind to try to deceive him or her.

One of the devil's favorite tricks is to lure the believer into the trap of offense. More people leave their local church over offense than anything else. Offense comes to the believer in seed form, then multiplies as the believer continues to rehearse it in his or her mind. When the offense grows large enough, the offended individual will look for ways to hurt the one who brought the offense. If they perceive that leaving will hurt the offender, so be it.

We've all had opportunities to be offended, and most have committed an offense at one time or another. Sometimes a person will put their "foot in their mouth" and say the wrong thing. If that person is conscientious—recognizing his or her mistake—they'll try to lessen the impact of their words by saying, "No offense." If the individual to whom they were speaking is a forgiving soul, they'll respond, "None taken." Pay careful attention to those two words. *None taken* is always the right response for the believer. Practice saying that a few times: "None taken." Let those words escape your lips the next time an offense presents itself.

If a person *can* be offended, they *will* be offended. Some people are offense-magnets, just looking for someone to wrong them. If they go too long without being offended, they'll fabricate an offense in their mind to carry around. Christians must determine to be people who cannot be offended. Say what you will, do what you want, spit at me or slap me, you're not going to get me to take offense. The believer must be adamant about resisting offense because offense can devastate a person's life. I know people who were offended decades ago and are still carrying around their offense. They've allowed their offense to make decisions for them, and some allow offense to dismiss them from God's plan for their lives.

If you're offended, that offense is hurting *your* life, not the life of the person who offended you. Get rid of it right away. Stop sulking and talking about it. I once heard a preacher say, "Taking offense is like drinking poison and expecting the other person to die." That offense will hurt *you*, taking your inner man to a place that's unreachable to everyone, including God.

> A brother offended is more unyielding than a strong city, and quarreling is like the bars of a castle.
>
> Proverbs 18:19

OFFENSE IN THE LOCAL CHURCH

The local church seems to be the easiest place in which to be offended. The greeter didn't give you a smile *and* a handshake, the music was too loud or too soft, the usher made you reach for the offering bucket, they left your name out of the list of birthdays in the church bulletin, etc. The person who allows themselves to be bothered by such trivialities is an easy target for the devil. The mature person, on the other hand, doesn't even notice such things.

As you serve in the Ministry of Helps, you'll work with others who may not have yet attained your level of sanctification. It's easy for offense to come as you're working alongside other people. How do you react when a person does a job differently than you'd do it? Can you just make the change and flow with them or do you mumble about how *nobody knows how to do anything right at this church?* Understand this: maturity brings flexibility. The spiritually mature person is adaptable and agreeable.

OFFENDED BY YOUR PASTOR

Believers in the local church receive the Word of God from their pastor. That's a wonderful thing but it can also be problematic in that there's great potential for offense. First, the pastor is human and may be prone to saying things that could be taken wrong (ask me how I know). Maybe the pastor even speaks in a way that seems abrasive. As his words combine with the anointing, they can come across in a way that's stronger than he realizes. Those words can have a piercing effect in the soul of the hearer.

Second, the Word itself can be offensive. The Bible speaks of *the offense of the cross* (Galatians 5:11). We've all heard of an offensive odor. That's when there's not just a mild smell, but one that stops you in your tracks. It confronts you and gets in your face. That's what the cross of Christ does: it confronts you and forces you to make a decision you don't want to make. The Word of God will sometimes get in your face in a way that's uncomfortable and unpleasant. Look at this description of the Word from Hebrews Chapter Four:

> For the word of God is living and active, **sharper than any two-edged sword**, piercing to the division of soul and of spirit, of joints and of marrow, and discerning the thoughts and intentions of the heart.
>
> Hebrews 4:12

I've been pierced, poked, sliced, and diced by the Word. I've had the Word of God step on all my toes at once. I wasn't sure if I was angry with the preacher or the Bible itself. (Many take offense at what the preacher says, not realizing he's just teaching what the Bible says.) My first thought might have been to be offended, but I had decided ahead of time that I wouldn't be. Here's another example from the Word:

> Yet hath he not root in himself, but endureth for a while: for when tribulation or persecution ariseth **because of the word, by and by he is offended.**
>
> Matthew 13:21 (KJV)

Since it's true that the Word of God can bring offense, how likely is it that offense will come through your pastor? After all, he's the one who most often brings you the Word. I would say we ought to *expect* to be offended by our pastor. What's more, that's not a bad thing; we should welcome it! When the Word gets in your face, it means you're standing in opposition to it—just like two people who are quarreling might stand face-to-face.

If I'm living in opposition to the Word of God, I *want* somebody or something to get in my face. I don't want to be so stubborn that my donkey has to sit down and speak to me like Balaam's did. I've had things in my life sit down and fall apart before. That's the time to get a clue and start making changes. If you refuse, things in your life will start talking to you (body parts, checkbooks, etc.) that shouldn't ordinarily be talking. Let's not get to that point.

I want to be corrected if I need to be corrected. And who better to bring that correction than my pastor? It may help the believer to say to themselves as they're being seated in church, "None taken. No matter what's spoken or done, I refuse to take offense." Let's grow in this area until we actually *embrace* offense—loving the correction, but resisting the bitter poison of indignation.

"Do you think the pastor's going to mention tithing again this week?" Bring it on! Bring it to me every week if you want. If it offends me, I'll make the needed changes. Here's a thought: preaching on tithing has never offended the tither. The one who takes offense is the non-tither, and the look of offense on his or her face is an advertisement to everyone that they're a non-tither. I'd hate to be a non-tither and would especially hate if everyone around could tell it!

DON'T GET MAD AT THE PASTOR

I've had people get so mad at me after I preached I thought they were going to attack me. After one particular service, a man pulled his entire family out of our church (I didn't find out until later, when I called to check up on him). He said my preaching had offended his family and they wouldn't be returning. He said they'd be looking for another church, where the preacher had some compassion. What he meant to say was that he was going to look for a church that omitted any truths that could be offensive. Those kinds of churches are easy to find. They're everywhere.

After that same service, another couple came to me and said, "Our home and family will never be the same because of what you preached today. We see exactly what adjustments to make and we're going to make them right away." I hadn't preached in a harsh or abusive manner. The issue was that one family was easily offended, while the other family had decided they couldn't be offended. Because they weren't offended, they were helped. Be the kind of person who refuses to take offense.

I told our church members ahead of time to expect offense to sometimes come to them through me. I also taught them to take the correction without taking the offense. If a pastor doesn't occasionally preach something that brings offense, I'd question whether they're really preaching the Word. That doesn't mean pastors are trying to offend anyone (believe me, anyone who's ever preached knows that you sometimes offend people without trying to). Pastors must do their best not to act or preach in an offensive or harsh manner. Strong, yes, but never harsh and void of the love of God.

Let's practice by saying this a few times: *none taken.*

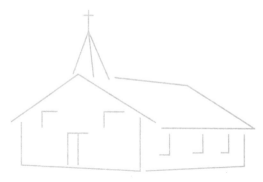

CHAPTER 20

Leaving the Local Church (and other really bad ideas)

When God joins a person to a local church, it's a holy thing, not an insignificant thing. The church to which He joins you is part of His plan for your life, and the fulfillment of that plan hinges on you being in your place. Sometimes, a person comes to Christ in a church that's sufficient for a season, but for that person to grow, they'll need to find a church that flows with the Word and the Spirit. That was the case in my life. I've only been a member of two different churches: the one I started in, and the one I was planted in after receiving the Baptism in the Holy Spirit.

When a person is planted in a strong local church, it's usually the will of God that they stay there throughout the course of their life (unless, of course, that person relocates to a different part of the country or world). When a believer goes around from church to church every few months or years, something's not right. God desires to *plant* the believer. He'll put you with the pastor that can best help you grow and mature.

A COVENANT RELATIONSHIP

The relationship between a believer and his or her church and pastor should be thought of as a covenant relationship. Any relationship that God establishes is a covenant relationship; it's the only kind He knows. The Lord never seeks a casual, noncommittal relationship, yet that's what exists between many believers and their local church.

Speaking of noncommittal, I'm reminded of a couple that visited our church when they moved to town. God's Spirit came upon them during praise and worship in such a powerful way that they both wept through that part of the service. The following week they returned and were again touched to the point of tears (here's a valuable lesson: if you start weeping during a worship service when nothing's wrong, it's likely that God's Spirit is upon you. He may be joining you to that person or place).

After their second visit, this man spoke with my wife. He explained that they had moved from a particular part of the country where he had been the pastor of a *non-church*. Yes, you read that correctly. A non-church. He said he had about four hundred people in this non-church. He explained that this kind of church was mostly unorganized (that describes a lot of churches I've seen); they had no building, no regular meetings, etc. I filled in the rest of the blanks: no tithing, no commitment, no accountability, no anointing, and so on.

He said he loved our service but was really looking for a non-church in our area. How does one go about finding one if they don't really exist? I suppose he found what he was looking for because he never returned. I'd share more about this but I admit I'm not entirely clear myself about the non-church. I guess that man was really a non-pastor (in fact, I'm sure of it). My point is, the non-church of which this man spoke knew nothing about covenant relationships.

One's local church should never be thought of as a come-and-go type of place. It's a much bigger deal than that, yet many view the local church with a convenience-store mentality. People want to come in, quickly get what they want, and leave. That's wrong on so many levels.

I recently visited with a distant relative whom I'd not seen in many years. As we spoke, I mentioned I was in ministry. This relative, claiming to be a Christian, began criticizing the pastor's message at a service he had attended. He explained that the message lacked entertainment value. He then informed me he only attends church once a year. I'd be upset too if I only heard one sermon a year and it wasn't entertaining. Like many so-called Christians, this man saw church as an optional, casual thing rather than a covenant relationship.

BREAKING COVENANT

A covenant relationship is where each party gives their all to the other. Marriage is an example of a covenant relationship. If people viewed their local church and pastor the way they viewed marriage, perhaps they wouldn't be as quick to leave. A revelation of this truth would help many people.

It should be a monumental decision to think about leaving the place in which God planted you. If a church relationship is like a marriage relationship, then leaving the church should be as grave a decision as leaving one's spouse. Having pastored for many years, I can say I know what it feels like to go through a divorce. No, I've never been previously married, but I've had many people with whom I was in covenant leave. It often hurts, not because of an emotional attachment, but because covenants are of the heart and are not to be broken.

A person contemplating leaving their church should try these words on for size: "I'm considering breaking covenant with my pastor and church family." Does leaving seem like the right thing to do when you think of it that way? It should be as unusual for a person to switch churches as it is for a tree to be pulled up and planted elsewhere. When a person leaves the church in which they were planted and goes to another church, it's a transplant. A transplant in the human body is a big deal and a spiritual transplant from one church to another is a big deal.

I'm not saying it's never right to leave a church. When I pastored, there were people who left in the will of God, but not many. There will always be those who move for school, work, etc. but even then, people need to seek God and the counsel of their pastor to ensure they're making the right move. We celebrated people who left the right way, but most who left should not have.

THE RIGHT WAY TO LEAVE

If you feel as though you must leave your local church, be careful how you handle it. If you're leaving because you feel it's the will of God (that's the only good reason to leave), speak with your pastor about what you're sensing. Be open to any counsel he may offer. He may say, "Yes, that sits well with me" or "I sensed that as well." On the other hand, he may say something like: "That doesn't seem right to me." "Please pray about this some more." "What you're planning doesn't agree with the Word of God."

Respect the wisdom of your pastor and give it your highest consideration. If you choose to leave anyway, that's your prerogative. In any case, whether you agree or disagree, let your pastor know your decision. Don't just disappear, leaving your pastor and church family wondering what happened to you. If you're not able to speak personally with the pastor, call the church office or send a letter or email: something to let the church know you're leaving.

If you're involved in the Ministry of Helps, give as much notice as possible so your position may be filled by someone with appropriate training and experience. It's not right to hurt a church on your way out by leaving a hole they have to scramble to fill. God will never lead a person to hurt their local church.

If there's anything I dislike, it's the person who leaves before they leave. By that I mean, once a person knows they're transitioning, they give minimal effort to everything they do. If you're leaving a place, be a strong finisher. It's more important to finish well than to start well. First impressions are important, but last impressions last. Every time I've vacated a ministry position, God has emphasized to me the importance of finishing strong. When the time came for me to go, the leaders I served knew I had given full effort all the way to the end.

WATCH YOUR MOUTH

If you're leaving without the blessing of your pastor, be sure not to speak ill of him or the church. No matter what issue is prompting your departure, let the issue be yours alone. There's no worse seed a person could sow than to spread discord among the members of a local church. The believer should be careful not to do or say anything that may influence other members of the church to also leave. If you must go, go quietly. God cares much for His church and will vigorously protect it.

Lastly, stay off the internet. You're not God's policeman or whistle-blower. He's not leading you to start a campaign to expose anyone. If your leader has fallen into sin, there are ways it can be dealt with discreetly and properly. Web pages that expose a minister's alleged indiscretions negatively affect the entire Body of Christ, cause younger believers to stumble, and can prevent a repentant leader from being restored. The danger with internet and social media is that things can be published very quickly—when people are boiling mad, for instance—and have the potential to stay around for a long time.

If you've had an unpleasant experience with your pastor or local church, understand that you still need a pastor and church. Ask God to lead you to your place of feeding. If He only deals with you about the church you've left, ask to return. These are serious issues for the believer. Decades of experience have taught me that most people who leave their church never find another. Many just quit altogether.

Churches are imperfect because people are involved and people are imperfect. Regardless of negative experiences you may have had, the local church is to remain an integral part of your life. There's nothing wrong with God's plan for today: His plan for strong local churches. No one will influence God to change His plan, and no one will persuade Him to excuse them from participation in His plan. Don't make excuses to stay out of church. Don't buy into the lie that you're the victim of "spiritual abuse" and should remain isolated. You're no victim, you're an overcomer! God will bring you to a place of restoration. Don't tell people, "I just need time away to heal." Get in church and be healed! Remember, God's plan is the local church, and He has a church for you.

CHAPTER 21

What to Bring to Church

I thirst for you, the living God. When can I go and
worship in your presence?

Psalm 42:2 (TEV)

Church should be the highlight of the week for the believer. The genuine excitement and thrill of meeting
with God compares with nothing else. I hear about vacations
that some people take and, although I believe in vacations,
the activities sound so empty because they have nothing
to do with God. I get fidgety if I'm not in church every few

days. The things people miss church for are, to me, some of the most boring things in the world. There's nothing as exciting as church.

> What then, brothers? When you come together, each one has a hymn, a lesson, a revelation, a tongue, or an interpretation. Let all things be done for building up.
>
> 1 Corinthians 14:26

The believer must come to church having prepared his or her heart for worship. Notice in the verse above that the people of God didn't just come to *get* something, they came to *bring* something: a spiritual supply. No, we don't always publicly minister the things in our heart, but we still come ready to add to the service rather than just coming to receive. Besides bringing a spiritual supply, there are other practical ways in which the believer can prepare for church.

Some years ago, my children prepared to attend a week-long camp with their church youth group. Prior to the trip, they were given a list entitled *Things to Bring to Camp*. There was also a section that specified what not to bring. My wife and I appreciated this list, as we had never before sent our children on such a trip.

After reading that list, I thought it would be great to have a list for Christians who come to church. This list wouldn't contain items such as underwear and socks, but would feature spiritual attitudes and attributes necessary for worship. Believers don't always bring what they should to the house of God. And sometimes, they bring things that should have been left at home. To help us all show up prepared, here's a list of items that no believer should be without:

Alarm Clock. Okay, this doesn't need to come to church, but many people obviously need one. Develop the habit of arriving early rather than late. When a person is consistently late to church, it indicates a casual attitude towards the things of God. If people are coming in late during the beginning of the service, it can affect the flow of the service in a major way. Don't be late to church!

Hunger. I don't like going to a restaurant unless I'm hungry. Food tastes different when you're hungry; it tastes better. Church is also better when a person is hungry. How does a person develop a hunger and thirst for the things of God? By partaking often of those things. The Bible speaks of eating His Words and drinking of His Spirit. The more you eat and drink, the more you want. It's similar to how an addict builds up tolerance and craves more of an addictive substance, except our addiction to the things of God will bless us, not kill us.

Receptivity. People who desire to receive from God are wonderful to minister to because their receptivity acts as a spiritual vacuum that pulls on God's anointing. When a minister stands before a congregation of receptive people, he will often tap into an additional measure of inspiration. When ministering to a receptive crowd, I often speak things that were not originally part of my message. Those things are a blessing to everyone.

Faith. It helps a minister when people are exercising faith for the service. When my wife and I attend special meetings, we prepare our hearts just as we would if we were ministering. There are things we say to each other before meetings as an expression of our faith. "I'll get all I came for" is a favorite saying of ours. Another is, "Everything that's supposed to happen will happen." If congregation members would bring faith to church services by believing and speaking similarly, our meetings would escalate in quality and results.

Fullness. It's one thing to have a church full of people; it's another thing to have full people in the church. If forced to choose between the two, I'd rather have the latter. There's no greater assist to a pastor than the believer who has learned to live full of God. Many church-goers live empty. Instead of bringing a spiritual supply to the service, their emptiness creates a spiritual void. If a high percentage of the congregation is spiritually lacking, it will have a draining effect on the service. The full person, on the other hand, helps lift the service to a higher level, enhancing the quality of ministry.

Willingness. If I sense that a person doesn't desire to help, I don't want their help. God's the same way. More important than the work we do is the attitude by which we perform it. God only rewards the willing heart (Isaiah 1:19); God only recognizes the willing gift (2 Corinthians 8:12, 9:7). Become the kind of person who is ever willing to serve.

Flexibility. Ministry is full of changes, and the people of God must remain adaptable. Don't be so married to your routine that you can't make changes when necessary. Being flexible in church will benefit your entire life, for the leadings of the Spirit we often receive also require flexibility. Be an easy-going, low-maintenance individual. Be honored to serve in any capacity. As a pastor, I always liked the people that were so thrilled to be saved that they didn't care where they served.

Hospitality. Each of us should consider ourselves ambassadors—representing God, the church, and the pastor. Although some may be appointed to serve in this area, all should make the welcoming of guests their personal responsibility. The hospitable person is always looking out for others and always reaching out. Such individuals bring a level of care to the local church that's valuable to God and the pastor. Hospitable people are effective soul-winners because they're not afraid to touch others with the love of God.

Excitement. Excitement can be contagious, and there's nothing more exciting than being where God is moving. It should be normal to see church-goers lit-up with excitement over what God has done and is about to do. Before I was saved, I met a Christian lady who was genuinely thrilled with the things of God. She wasn't pushy with her beliefs, yet the excitement she had for her new life made an impression on me that factored into my decision to receive Christ.

> When they said, "Let's go to the house of God," my heart leaped for joy.
>
> Psalm 122:1 (MSG)

Smile. While some in the church may have not yet learned to cast their cares upon the Lord, it should never be the case that the majority of the congregation looks sad or downcast. Heaven is a happy place, and the local church should reflect Heaven's joy. If you don't normally smile, be sure to put one on when you come to church. Your smile may be the encouragement that someone else needs.

Tithe. Everyone can be a tither and giver. A person shouldn't think of coming to church without tithes and offerings any more than they would think to come without their clothes. The believer's tithe is more than just a necessary item of business; it's part of the worship experience.

Bible and Notebook. It's surprising how many people come to church with no practical way to retain what's being ministered. Having your Bible present to highlight or notate is important. The believer who desires to put God's Word into practice may also want to take notes for later reference. This is all part of coming to church prepared to receive.

Pacifier. I'm not speaking about keeping your crying baby quiet (although that's appreciated). Many Christians fail to recognize the need to control their *own* mouths when coming to church. Whining and words of doubt certainly don't belong at church, but there are also other ways in which believers must monitor their mouths. In particular, we must guard against an overabundance of words as we converse with others prior to a service.

When right words are spoken in the house of God, they help create a positive spiritual atmosphere. Conversely, too much natural, trivial conversation can hinder the flow of a service. We must bring reverence to our worship services. That doesn't mean people must sit in silence as they wait for the service to begin. We should be friendly, outgoing, and loving toward others, all the while keeping our hearts turned toward God. After the service, when the Word has been received, is a good time to catch up on the life-events of others.

Most Christians love their church family and eagerly anticipate seeing their brothers and sisters in the Lord. This desire for fellowship is a godly thing and meaningful conversations with others are to be encouraged. The area I'm speaking of is the contribution all can make to an atmosphere of worship. If your tendency is to be overly chatty before a service, insert your spiritual pacifier by turning your heart toward God and communing with Him.

> As you enter the house of God, keep your ears open
> and your mouth shut. . . .
>
> Ecclesiastes 5:1 (NLT)

The next time you're getting ready for church, pack all these items to bring along. You can leave apathy, distraction, un-teachableness, and selfishness at home. They're not welcome in the church. Neither are gossip, a critical spirit, stinginess, or other poor attitudes. If you'd prefer not to be in church, *make* yourself want to be there. Take yourself by the ear and tell yourself to get happy and get involved. It won't be long until your excitement is genuine and you'll be one of the biggest blessings in the building.

CHAPTER 22

How to Find the Right Church

W hich church you attend is a matter of great importance. When a child is born, in most cases he or she already has a home with loving parents. Think of the child's chances for survival were this not the case. Every Christian also needs a good church home if he or she is to grow and thrive. Finding that right place can seem like a daunting task, but it need not be difficult. Here are some tips to help you find the right church:

• Pray, asking God to lead you to the right place.

• Realize that He already has a good church for you. Because we live in a world where we're accustomed to making choices, it's tempting to make our own decision where to attend rather than discovering God's plan for our lives.

• Be willing to go anywhere God leads, even if it doesn't initially look like what you had in mind. Set your preference aside. It's not "What do I like?" but "What does God have for me?"

• Once you're certain you're in the right place, there's no need to look further. Don't fall into the trap of church-hopping or you'll miss much of what God has for you.

• Don't make the mistake of looking for the perfect church. As someone has said, "The only perfect church is the church with no people." Even the pastor, though gifted to lead and teach, is still human and can make mistakes from time to time.

• God will lead you to a place that places a high emphasis on His Word (the Bible). If you don't need a Bible in a particular church, be assured it's not the church for you.

• God will lead you to a place where the people worship freely and the Holy Spirit's work is recognized and welcomed.

• God will lead you to a place where the people are warm and loving and you're made to feel welcome.

Most of all, when you're in the place God wants you, it will seem like home. Now, get involved and be as supportive as you know how to be. Adapt to your church and pastor; don't try to make them adapt to you. Congratulations on finding your God-ordained place. Welcome home!

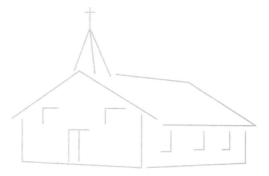

CHAPTER 23

Fat and Flourishing

The righteous shall flourish like the palm tree: he shall grow like a cedar in Lebanon. Those that be planted in the house of the Lord shall flourish in the courts of our God. They shall still bring forth fruit in old age; they shall be fat and flourishing; To show that the Lord is upright: he is my rock, and there is no unrighteousness in him.

Psalm 92:12-15 (KJV)

God desires that His children be abundantly blessed; however, His blessing doesn't just flow anywhere. The blessing of the Lord meets the believer as he or she is planted in the house of the Lord: the local church. Everything about our lives ought to be better because of our church. Some allow themselves to be pulled away from their place, but the believer who remains in *the courts of our God*—the place where He works and moves—will flourish throughout their lifetime.

STRONG AS A PALM

I grew up in South Florida, just a few blocks from the Atlantic Ocean. In the yard of our house were several palm trees. Palm trees are unique in that there are no branches protruding along the length of the trunk, just the foliage on top. It would appear such a tree would be weak and exposed, but the opposite is true.

The coasts of Florida have been ground-zero for many hurricanes. These storms can rip the roofs off houses, but they can't easily uproot a palm tree. The lack of branches combined with deep roots make it a very difficult tree to uproot. Besides that, palm trees are so flexible that they can actually bend over and touch the ground under the intense pressure of a storm. When the storm subsides, the palm tree springs right back up to its vertical position. It's an amazing tree.

The Christian who remains planted in the house of God

(the local church) will flourish *like the palm tree*, Scripture says. They may weather some storms and go through some difficulties, but their deep roots allow them to maintain victory and just spring right back up.

Growing up, I remember watching television advertisements for a toy called the *Weeble*. The Weeble looked just like a person, but instead of having legs and feet, Weebles had a weighted round base. If you tried to knock over the Weeble, it would spring right back up. The advertising slogan for this toy was "Weebles wobble but they don't fall down." Like the palm tree and the Weeble, the storms of life simply cannot upend the church-loving Christian. The enemy may get in some shots and knock them backward, but when it looks like they're going down, they're really just gathering momentum for their upswing. It's a stupid devil who tries to mess with the believer who's properly planted. No matter what happens, that believer will not go down and will not go away.

PLANTED FOR PROSPERITY

I believe strongly in faith and Biblical prosperity and have made those subjects areas of continual study in my life. Our passage in Psalm 92 reveals a connection between the local church and the believer's prosperity; prosperity flows to the believer as long as he or she remains planted. As clear as

Scripture is on this subject, many still fail to grasp the truth. I've met people—far more than I can number—whose neglect of the local church has caused their needs to go unmet. These individuals may have been dedicated to Christ—faithful to confess the Word and sow financial seeds—but that's only part of the equation. One cannot violate the spiritual law which requires the believer to be properly planted.

God's a good builder. He won't build a person's life higher than the foundation of that life will support. If we desire to greatly increase, we must plant deep roots. The local church is where Christians put down their roots. It's a garden in which believers may grow. We must not make the mistake of viewing prosperity and blessing independently of the local church.

BODY PROBLEMS

When my wife and I pastored in New York, we received many phone calls from people who said they were inquiring about our church. In most cases, we discovered that they really just wanted to talk about their problems. We would explain to them that our church phone number wasn't a counseling line and would encourage them to visit the church in person, at which time we'd be glad to speak with them.

During those same years, I also appeared on a television show where people called in questions to be answered by a panel of pastors. They were supposed to be asking questions about the Bible, but again, they often called about their personal problems.

Between the calls at church and those on the TV show, I heard a lot of people describe their problems. After several years, I asked my wife, "Have you noticed that all these problems can be traced back to one issue?" She agreed I was correct. Although their problems manifested in a variety of areas (marriage, family, health, financial, emotional, etc.), there was really only one root issue: most of these people were not in church and were therefore out of their place in the Body. They had what I call *Body problems*.

The easiest way to get out of place in the Body of Christ is to be uprooted from one's local church. Uprooting, however, should not be a simple task. It should be as difficult to uproot the believer from his or her church as it is to uproot a tree from the ground. If a person is easily uprooted, it means their roots never ran deep to begin with; they were never firmly planted. People who are out of place in Christ's Body will have problems in many other areas, including their physical body. In these cases, it's not an issue of healing as much as it's an issue of them getting back in their place.

I estimate that ninety percent of the problems people spoke to us about were these Body problems. I would tell people that their answer was to find and become planted in their place of feeding: the local church. Was my counsel heeded? Sadly, no. I'm not aware of even one instance where my encouragement was received and acted upon. Sometimes the person would become angry, thinking that I was ignoring their real issues and trying to persuade them to attend our church. They were convinced that their spouse was their problem, or that it was a money or physical issue. No. They had Body problems and would never flourish until they became planted in their God-assigned place.

It would be ridiculous to pull a tree out of the ground and then wonder why it was declining in health. It's just as crazy for a Christian to pull themselves out of their local church and then wonder why they're not prospering. Stay planted and stay strong.

LEAVING A LEGACY

> They shall still bring forth fruit in old age; they shall be fat and flourishing; To show that the Lord is upright. . . .
>
> Psalm 92:14-15

I'm not interested in my life being cut short because I failed to remain in my place. Nor do I want the lives of others cut off when their wisdom and experience are needed most. This verse specifies *old age* as one blessing of the person who spends their days in the local church. We need those who are older to be an example to those who are younger. We need the testimonies of those who have borne eternal fruit for God's kingdom. We should be able to go to the local church and see rows of people who have been there a long time and are thriving, fruitful, and blessed.

The lives of those who are fat and flourishing reflect the goodness of God. We should aspire to be like those who have experienced a lifetime of God's faithfulness. Purpose to spend your days in the local church. Stay planted. Stay plugged in. Flourish like the palm tree and leave a legacy that can be followed by the saplings: multitudes of new believers who are springing up in our day.

Salvation

The most important decision you can make in life is the decision to receive Jesus Christ as your personal Lord and Savior. It is a decision to turn from sin and self, and to follow God, every day and in every way.

This decision to receive Christ is what the Bible calls being *born again*, or being *saved*. Without this salvation experience, people are doomed to failure in life and eternity in hell. Success and eternal life belong to the believer in Christ. If you have been reading this book and don't know that you have been born-again, it's time to make the decision to follow Christ.

Read what God says in His word about this great experi-ence:

> Truly, truly, I say to you, whoever hears my word and believes him who sent me has eternal life. He does not come into judgment, but has passed from death to life.
>
> John 5:24

> For God so loved the world, that he gave his only Son, that whoever believes in him should not perish but have eternal life. For God did not send his Son into the world to condemn the world, but in order that the world might be saved through him.
>
> John 3:16-17

> For by grace you have been saved through faith. And this is not your own doing; it is the gift of God, not a result of works, so that no one may boast.
>
> Ephesians 2:8-9

> If you confess with your mouth that Jesus is Lord and believe in your heart that God raised him from the dead, you will be saved. For with the heart one believes and is justified, and with the mouth one confesses and is saved.
>
> Romans 10:9-10

Because our sin has separated us from God, we need a Savior, one who would take our place in eternal death and give us eternal life. Jesus is that Savior; the only one qualified to take our place.

> And this is the testimony, that God gave us eternal life, and this life is in his Son. Whoever has the Son has life; whoever does not have the Son of God does not have life.

> 1 John 5:11-12

Receive Christ right now by praying a prayer such as this one. Speak the words from your heart, and God will hear and answer you.

> Dear God, I see that my sins have separated me from You, and I repent of sin. Thank You that you loved me so much that You sent Jesus to suffer and die on my behalf, so that I could receive eternal life. I believe Jesus died for me and rose again, and I receive Him as my Savior right now. Jesus, You are my Lord, and I'll live for You from this day on. Thank You, Father, for saving me!

If you prayed that prayer and meant it, be assured that God has done exactly what you asked. You are now His child. You have been born into His family. This verse now describes you, the new creation:

> Therefore, if anyone is in Christ, he is a new creation.
> The old has passed away; behold, the new has come.

2 Corinthians 5:17

There are some additional steps you should take now that you are a follower of Jesus Christ. The most important step is to find a good local church. The pastor there will minister to you and help you grow in the things of God. Make sure your church believes and teaches the Bible and allows the Holy Spirit to work freely. Your pastor can help teach you about other steps to get started in the Christian life, such as studying the Word of God, being filled with the Holy Spirit, tithing, and serving in the local church.

Congratulations on making life's most important decision!

About the Author

Faith in God's Word, and constant reliance on the Holy Spirit have been the keys to success in the life and ministry of Rev. Joel Siegel. Raised and educated as a Jew, Joel Siegel, at age 18, had a life-transforming encounter with Christ that brought him true purpose and fulfillment.

Rev. Siegel began preaching and teaching the Word of God soon after he was saved in 1986. He entered full-time ministry in 1990, serving for three years as the music director for the gospel music group *Truth*. Truth's road schedule took Joel and his wife Amy worldwide to over 300 cities a year, ministering in churches and on college campuses.

From 1993 to 2000, Joel was the musical director for Rev. Kenneth E. Hagin's RHEMA Singers & Band. In addition to assisting Rev. Hagin in his crusade meetings, Joel produced eight music projects for the ministry, including his first solo release, *Trust & Obey*.

From 2000 to 2011, Joel and Amy (herself a skilled minister and worship leader), served as the founding pastors of Good News Family Church in Orchard Park, NY. During this time, they were frequently asked to host shows for the TCT Christian Television Network. Joel regularly hosted their popular *Ask The Pastor* program.

Rev. Siegel spends his time ministering to congregations in the U.S. and abroad, passionately endeavoring to fulfill his assignment to help lead this generation into the move of God that will usher in the return of Christ.

The Siegels make their home in Colorado. Joel oversees Faith Church Colorado in the town of Castle Rock, where Amy is lead pastor.

For music recordings, audio teaching series, books, and other resources, or to invite Rev. Joel to minister at a church or event, please visit www.joelsiegel.org.